WINDOWS™ 3.1

by: maranGraphics' Development Group

IDG Books Worldwide, Inc.
An International Data Group Company

San Mateo, California ✦ Indianapolis, Indiana ✦ Boston, Massachusetts

Windows™ 3.1 Visual PocketGuide

Published by
IDG Books Worldwide, Inc.
An International Data Group Company
155 Bovet Road, Suite 310
San Mateo, CA 94402
(415) 312-0650

Library of Congress Catalog Card No.: 94-079416

ISBN: 1-56884-650-9

Printed in the United States of America

10 9 8 7 6 5 4 3 2 1

Distributed in the United States by IDG Books Worldwide, Inc.

Distributed by Computer and Technical Books in Miami, Florida, for South America and the Caribbean; by Longman Singapore in Singapore, Malaysia, Thailand, and Korea; by Toppan Co. Ltd. in Japan; by Asia Computerworld in Hong Kong; by Woodslane Pty. Ltd. in Australia and New Zealand; and by Transworld Publishers Ltd. in the U.K. and Ireland.

For general information on IDG Books in the U.S., including information on discounts and premiums, contact IDG Books at 800-762-2974 or 317-895-5200.

For U.S. Corporate Sales and quantity discounts, contact maranGraphics at 800-469-6616, ext. 206.

For information on international sales of IDG Books, contact Christina Turner at 415-312-0633.

For information on translations, contact Marc Jeffrey Mikulich, Foreign Rights Manager, at IDG Books Worldwide. Fax Number 415-286-2747.

For sales inquiries and special prices for bulk quantities, write to the address above or call IDG Books Worldwide at 415-312-0650.

For information on using IDG Books in the classroom, or ordering examination copies, contact Jim Kelly at 800-434-2086.

Trademark Acknowledgments

maranGraphics Inc. has attempted to include trademark information for products, services and companies referred to in this guide. Although maranGraphics Inc. has made reasonable efforts in gathering this information, it cannot guarantee its accuracy.

Hewlett-Packard, DeskJet, and LaserJet are registered trademarks of Hewlett-Packard Company.

Microsoft, MS-DOS, and Microsoft Mouse are registered trademarks and Windows is a trademark of Microsoft Corporation.

Microsoft Paintbrush is a trademark of ZSoft Corporation.

Microsoft TrueType is a registered trademark of Apple Computer Corporation.

U.S. Corporate Sales

Contact maranGraphics at (800) 469-6616, ext. 206 or Fax (905) 890-9434.

U.S. Trade Sales

Contact IDG Books at (800) 434-3422 or (415) 312-0650.

About IDG Books Worldwide

Welcome to the world of IDG Books Worldwide.

IDG Books Worldwide, Inc., is a subsidiary of International Data Group, the world's largest publisher of business and computer-related information and the leading global provider of information services on information technology. IDG was founded more than 25 years ago and now employs more than 5,700 people worldwide. IDG publishes more than 200 computer publications in 63 countries (see listing below). Forty million people read one or more IDG publications each month.

Launched in 1990, IDG Books is today the fastest-growing publisher of computer and business books in the United States. We are proud to have received 3 awards from the Computer Press Association in recognition of editorial excellence, and our best-selling ...For Dummies series has more than 10 million copies in print with translations in more than 20 languages. IDG Books, through a recent joint venture with IDG's Hi-Tech Beijing, became the first U.S. publisher to publish a computer book in the People's Republic of China. In record time, IDG Books has become the first choice for millions of readers around the world who want to learn how to better manage their businesses.

Our mission is simple: Every IDG book is designed to bring extra value and skill-building instructions to the reader. Our books are written by experts who understand and care about our readers. The knowledge base of our editorial staff comes from years of experience in publishing, education, and journalism — experience which we use to produce books for the '90s. In short, we care about books, so we attract the best people. We devote special attention to details such as audience, interior design, use of icons, and illustrations. And because we use an efficient process of authoring, editing, and desktop publishing our books electronically, we can spend more time ensuring superior content and spend less time on the technicalities of making books.

You can count on our commitment to deliver high-quality books at competitive prices on topics customers want to read about. At IDG, we value quality, and we have been delivering quality for more than 25 years. You'll find no better book on a subject than an IDG book.

John Kilcullen
President and CEO
IDG Books Worldwide, Inc.

IDG Books Worldwide, Inc., is a subsidiary of International Data Group. The officers are Patrick J. McGovern, Founder and Board Chairman; Walter Boyd, President. International Data Group's publications include: ARGENTINA'S Computerworld Argentina, Infoworld Argentina; AUSTRALIA'S Computerworld Australia, Australian PC World, Australian Macworld, Network World, Mobile Business Australia, Reseller, IDG Sources; AUSTRIA'S Computerwelt Oesterreich, PC Test; BRAZIL'S Computerworld, Gamepro, Game Power, Mundo IBM, Mundo Unix, PC World, Super Game; BELGIUM'S Data News (CW) BULGARIA'S Computerworld Bulgaria, Ediworld, PC & Mac World Bulgaria, Network World Bulgaria; CANADA'S CIO Canada, Computerworld Canada, Graduate Computerworld, InfoCanada, Network World Canada; CHILE'S Computerworld Chile, Informatica; COLOMBIA'S Computerworld Colombia, PC World; CZECH REPUBLIC'S Computerworld, Elektronika, PC World; DENMARK'S Communications World, Computerworld Danmark, Macintosh Produktkatalog, Macworld Danmark, PC World Danmark, PC World Produktguide, Tech World, Windows World; ECUADOR'S PC World Ecuador; EGYPT'S Computerworld (CW) Middle East, PC World Middle East; FINLAND'S MikroPC, Tietoviikko, Tietoverkko; FRANCE'S Distributique, GOLDEN MAC, InfoPC, Languages & Systems, Le Guide du Monde Informatique, Le Monde Informatique, Telecoms & Reseaux; GERMANY'S Computerwoche, Computerwoche Focus, Computerwoche Extra, Computerwoche Karriere, Information Management, Macwelt, Netzwelt, PC Welt, PC Woche, Publish, Unit; GREECE'S Infoworld, PC Games; HUNGARY'S Computerworld SZT, PC World; HONG KONG'S Computerworld Hong Kong, PC World Hong Kong; INDIA'S Computers & Communications; IRELAND'S ComputerScope; ISRAEL'S Computerworld Israel, PC World Israel; ITALY'S Computerworld Italia, Lotus Magazine, Macworld Italia, Networking Italia, PC Shopping, PC World Italia; JAPAN'S Computerworld Today, Information Systems World, Macworld Japan, Nikkei Personal Computing, SunWorld Japan, Windows World; KENYA'S East African Computer News; KOREA'S Computerworld Korea, Macworld Korea, PC World Korea; MEXICO'S Compu Edicion, Compu Manufactura, Computacion/Punto de Venta, Computerworld Mexico, MacWorld, Mundo Unix, PC World, Windows; THE NETHERLANDS' Computer! Totaal, Computable (CW), LAN Magazine, MacWorld, Totaal "Windows"; NEW ZEALAND'S Computer Listings, Computerworld New Zealand, New Zealand PC World, Network World; NIGERIA'S PC World Africa; NORWAY'S Computerworld Norge, C/World, Lotusworld Norge, Macworld Norge, Networld, PC World Ekspress, PC World Norge, PC World's Produktguide, Publish& Multimedia World, Student Data, Unix World, Windowsworld; IDG Direct Response; PAKISTAN'S PC World Pakistan; PANAMA'S PC World Panama; PERU'S Computerworld Peru, PC World; PEOPLE'S REPUBLIC OF CHINA'S China Computerworld, China Infoworld, Electronics Today/Multimedia World, Electronics International, Electronic Product World, China Network World, PC and Communications Magazine, PC World China, Software World Magazine, Telecom Product World; IDG HIGH TECH BEIJING'S New Product World; IDG SHENZHEN'S Computer News Digest; PHILIPPINES' Computerworld Philippines, PC Digest (PCW); POLAND'S Computerworld Poland, PC World/Komputer; PORTUGAL'S Cerebro/PC World, Correio Informatico/Computerworld, Informatica & Comunicacoes Catalogo, MacIn, Nacional de Produtos; ROMANIA'S Computerworld, PC World; RUSSIA'S Computerworld-Moscow, Mir - PC, Sety; SINGAPORE'S Computerworld Southeast Asia, PC World Singapore; SLOVENIA'S Monitor Magazine; SOUTH AFRICA'S Computer Mail (CIO),Computing S.A.,Network World S.A., Software World; SPAIN'S Advanced Systems, Amiga World, Computerworld Espana, Communicaciones World, Macworld Espana, NeXTWORLD, Super Juegos Magazine (GamePro), PC World Espana, Publish; SWEDEN'S Attack, ComputerSweden, Corporate Computing, Natverk & Kommunikation, Macworld, Mikrodatorn, PC World, Publishing & Design (CAP), DataIngenjoren, Maxi Data,Windows World; SWITZERLAND'S Computerworld Schweiz, Macworld Schweiz, PC Tip; TAIWAN'S Computerworld Taiwan, PC World Taiwan; THAILAND'S Thai Computerworld; TURKEY'S Computerworld Monitor, Macworld Turkiye, PC World Turkiye; UKRAINE'S Computerworld; UNITED KINGDOM'S Computing /Computerworld, Connexion/Network World, Lotus Magazine, Macworld, Open Computing/Sunworld; UNITED STATES' Advanced Systems, AmigaWorld, Cable in the Classroom, CD Review, CIO, Computerworld, Digital Video, DOS Resource Guide, Electronic Entertainment Magazine, Federal Computer Week, Federal Integrator, GamePro, IDG Books, Infoworld, Infoworld Direct, Laser Event, Macworld, Multimedia World, Network World, PC Letter, PC World, PlayRight, Power PC World, Publish, SWATPro, Video Event; VENEZUELA'S Computerworld Venezuela, PC World; VIETNAM'S PC World Vietnam

Acknowledgments

Thanks to John Hodgins, Elliot Katz, and Allan Watson of Microsoft Canada Inc. for their support and consultation.

Special thanks to Wendi B. Ewbank for her patience, insight and humor throughout the project.

Thanks to the dedicated staff of maranGraphics including, Peters Ezers, David de Haas, David Hendricks, Jill Maran, Judy Maran, Maxine Maran, Robert Maran, Dave Ross, Christie Van Duin, Carol Walthers and Kelleigh Wing.

Finally, to Richard Maran who originated the easy-to-use graphic format of this guide. Thank you for your inspiration and guidance.

Credits

Author:
Ruth Maran

Consultant:
Wendi Blouin Ewbank

Layout Artist:
Carol Walthers

Designer:
David de Haas

Illustrator:
Dave Ross

Production Editor:
Kelleigh Wing

Editor:
Judy Maran

Post Production:
Robert Maran

TABLE OF CONTENTS

Getting Started

Windows Basics

Manage Your Applications

Manage Your Directories

TABLE OF CONTENTS

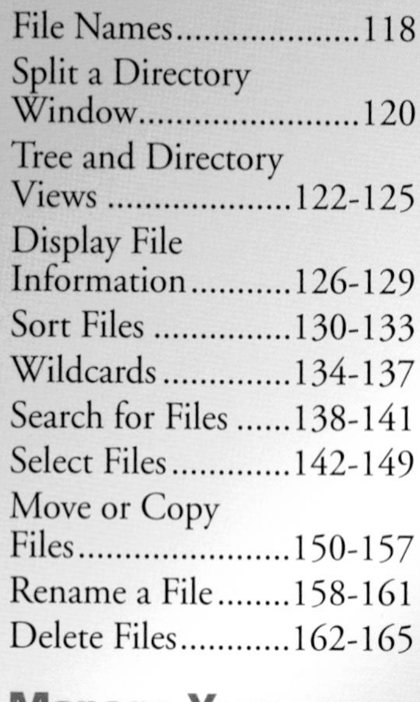

Manage Your Files

Manage Your Diskettes

Write

Print

Control Panel

Windows works with MS-DOS to maintain control over your computer. Like a traffic cop, Windows ensures your computer runs smoothly and efficiently.

Applications perform tasks such as word processing and spreadsheet analysis. Windows controls how these applications input and output their data.

Note: The terms program and application are used interchangeably.

Windows controls how an application interacts with you.

Windows provides tools to store and organize the files on your computer.

START WINDOWS

Start Windows

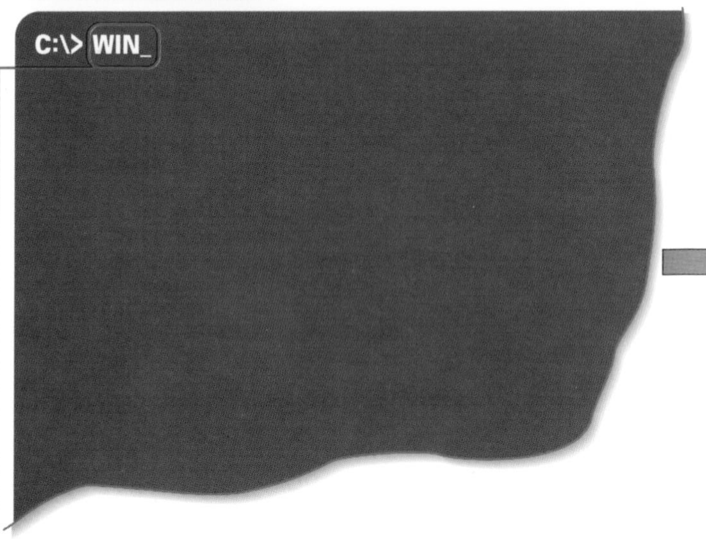

1 To start Microsoft® Windows™ 3.1 from MS-DOS, type **WIN** and then press Enter .

Tips:

◆ Windows 3.1 is installed on your hard drive in a directory named WINDOWS.

◆ You are using a mouse with Windows 3.1.

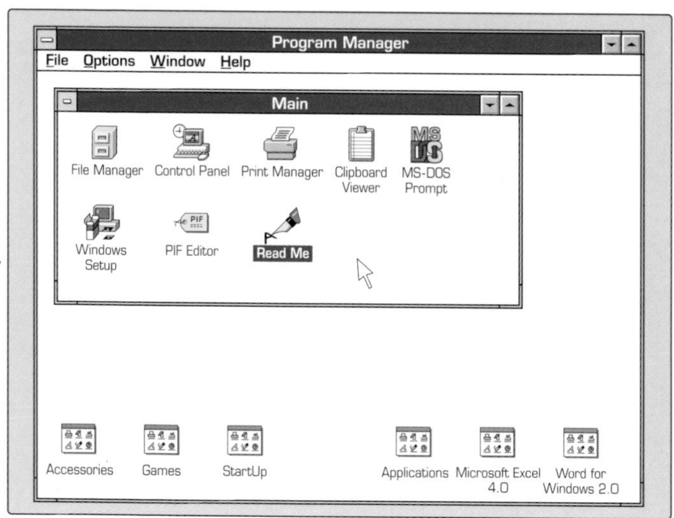

◆ The **Program Manager** window appears.

THE PROGRAM MANAGER

The Program Manager

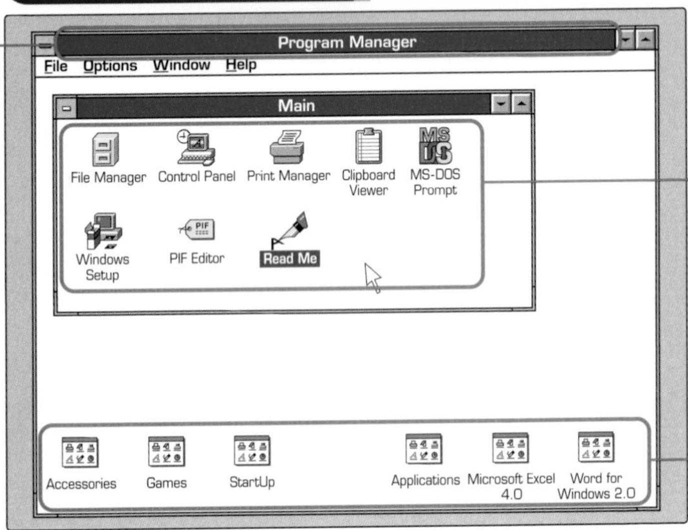

◆ Each time you start Windows, the **Program Manager** window appears.

Tips:

- An **icon** is a graphic that represents an application, a document or any other element.
- A **window** is a rectangle on your screen that contains icons or displays a document.

The Program Manager window contains two types of icons:

- A **program-item icon** represents a program that you can start from Windows (example: **File Manager**).
- A **group icon** organizes programs into groups (example: **Games**). A group icon can contain up to 50 program-item icons.

USING THE MOUSE

Using the Mouse

Hold the mouse as shown in the diagram. Your thumb and two rightmost fingers guide the mouse while your two remaining fingers press the mouse buttons.

Note: You can also use the mouse with your left hand. To change mouse settings, refer to page 240.

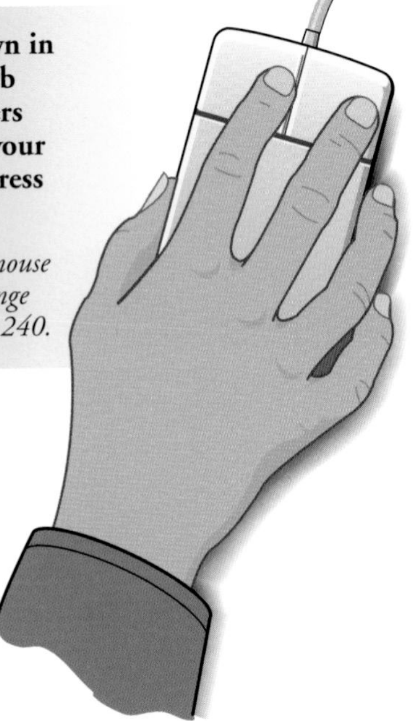

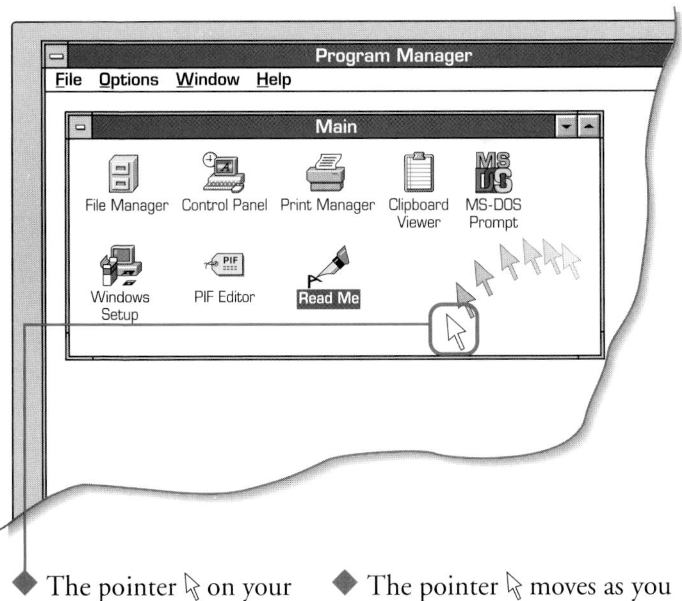

◆ The pointer ↖ on your screen represents the mouse.

◆ The pointer ↖ moves as you move the mouse. For example, the pointer ↖ moves down as you move the mouse down.

USING THE MOUSE

Parts of the Mouse

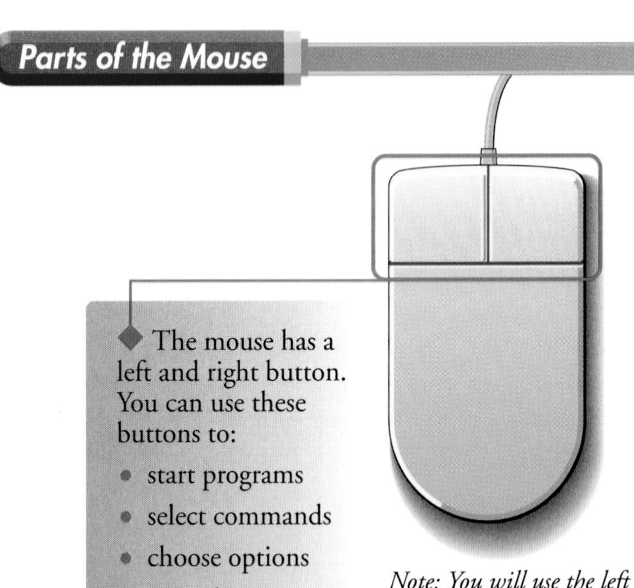

The mouse has a left and right button. You can use these buttons to:

- start programs
- select commands
- choose options
- move icons

Note: You will use the left button most of the time.

Mouse Terms

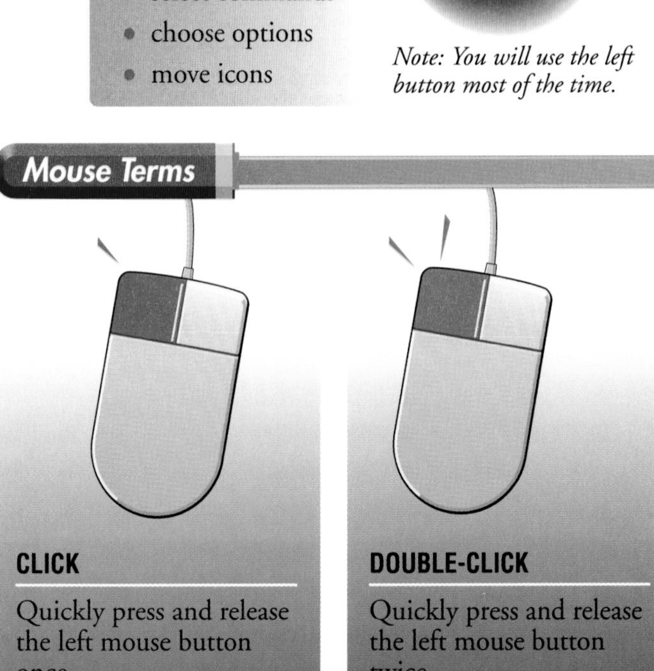

CLICK

Quickly press and release the left mouse button once.

DOUBLE-CLICK

Quickly press and release the left mouse button twice.

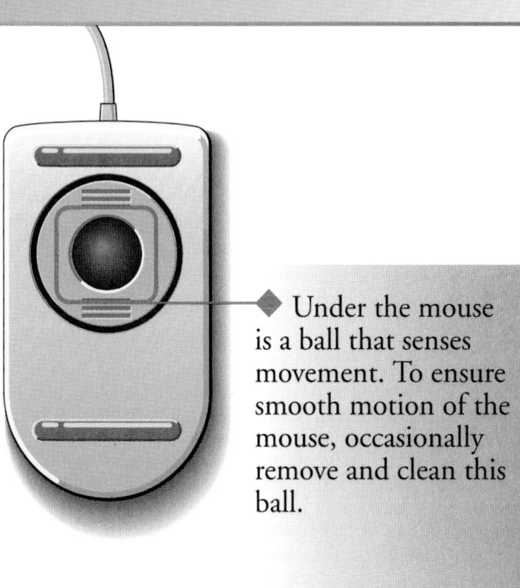

Under the mouse is a ball that senses movement. To ensure smooth motion of the mouse, occasionally remove and clean this ball.

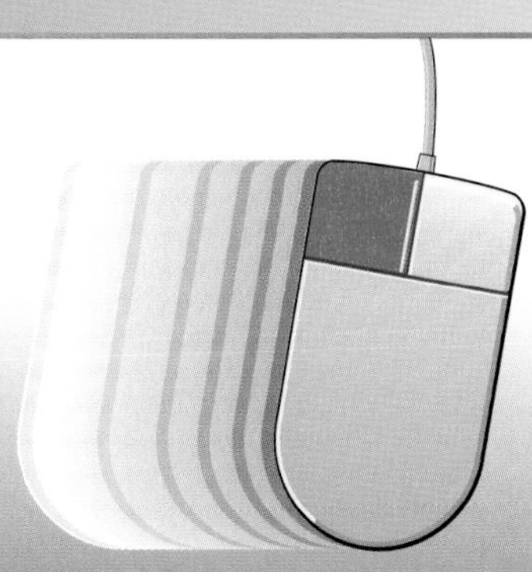

DRAG

When the mouse pointer is over an object on your screen, press and hold down the left mouse button and then move the mouse.

USING THE MENUS

Using the Menus

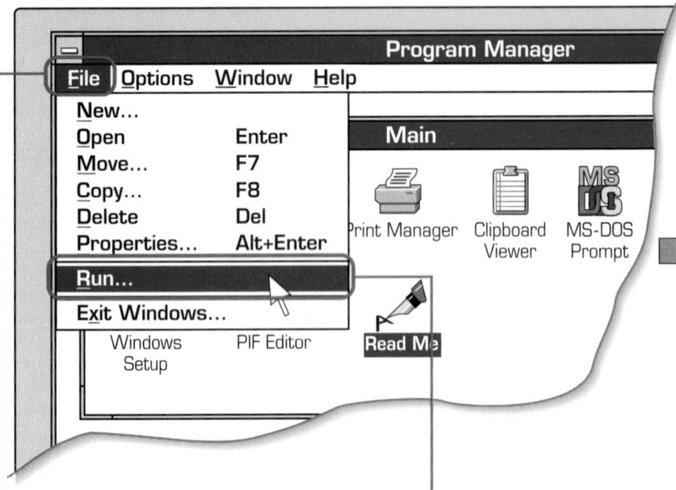

1 To open a menu, move the mouse over the menu name (example: **File**) and then press the left button.

Note: To close a menu, move the mouse anywhere outside the menu and then press the left button.

2 To select a command, move the mouse over the command name (example: **Run**) and then press the left button.

DIMMED COMMANDS

◆ If a command appears dimmed, it is currently unavailable.

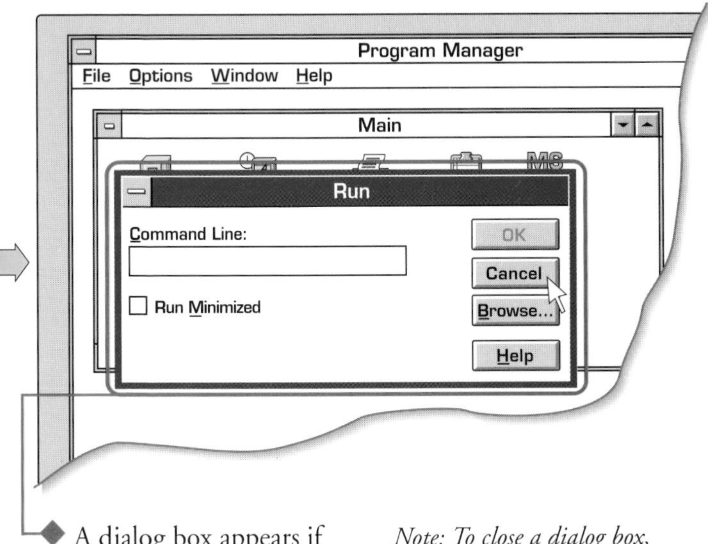

◆ A dialog box appears if Windows requires more information in order to carry out the command.

*Note: To close a dialog box, move the mouse over **Cancel** and then press the left button.*

USING THE KEYBOARD

Using the Keyboard

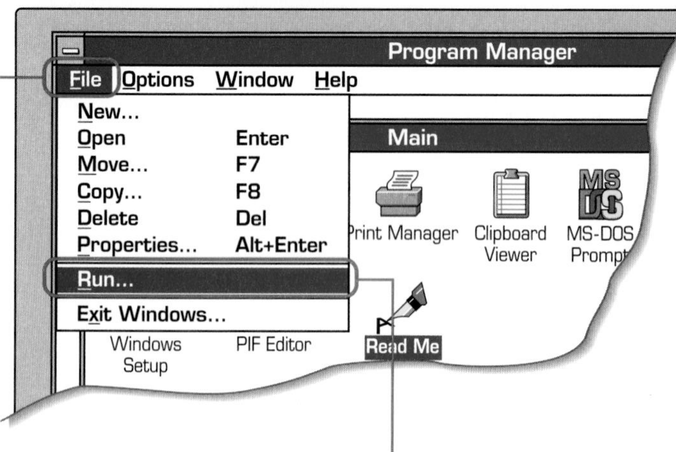

1 To open a menu, press Alt followed by the underlined letter in the menu name (example: F for **File**).

Note: To close a menu, press Alt.

2 To select a command, press the underlined letter in the command name (example: R for **Run**).

Note: To close a dialog box, press Esc.

Tip:

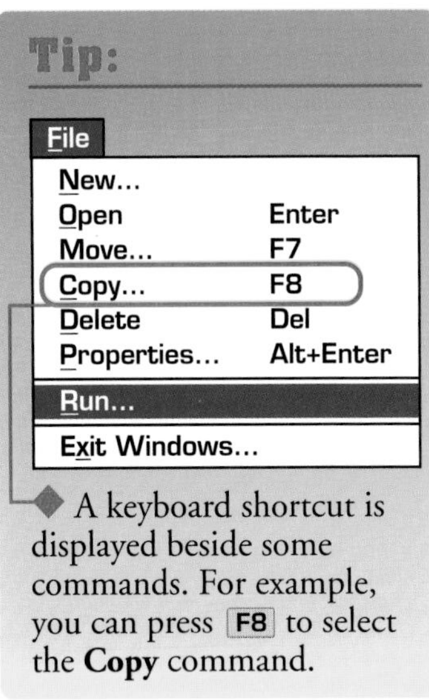

◆ A keyboard shortcut is displayed beside some commands. For example, you can press F8 to select the **Copy** command.

KEY COMBINATIONS

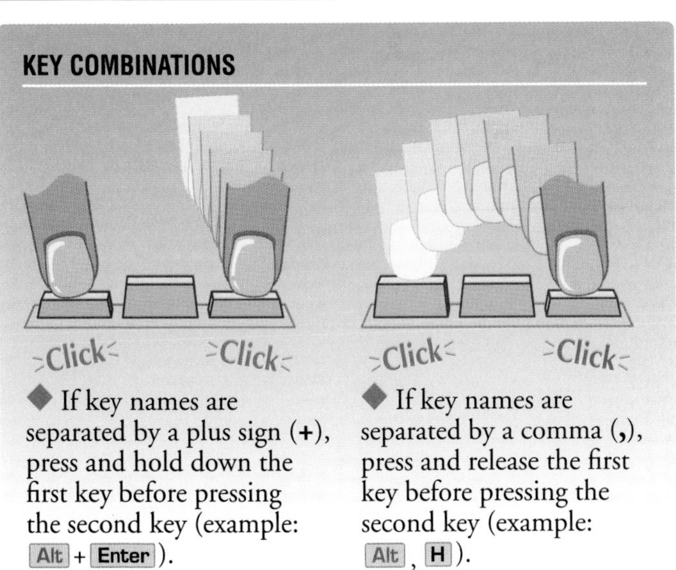

◆ If key names are separated by a plus sign (**+**), press and hold down the first key before pressing the second key (example: Alt + Enter).

◆ If key names are separated by a comma (**,**), press and release the first key before pressing the second key (example: Alt , H).

SAVE SETTINGS ON EXIT

Save Settings on Exit

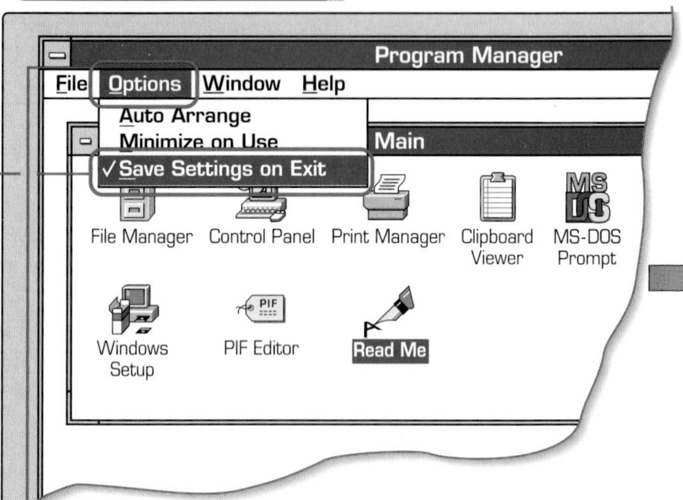

1 Move the mouse over **Options** and then press the left button.

◆ A check mark (✓) displayed beside **Save Settings on Exit** indicates the command is **on**.

2 To leave the command on, press Alt to close the **Options** menu.

*Note: To turn the command **off**, move the mouse over **Save Settings on Exit** and then press the left button.*

You can save the last arrangement of windows and icons on your screen when you exit Windows.

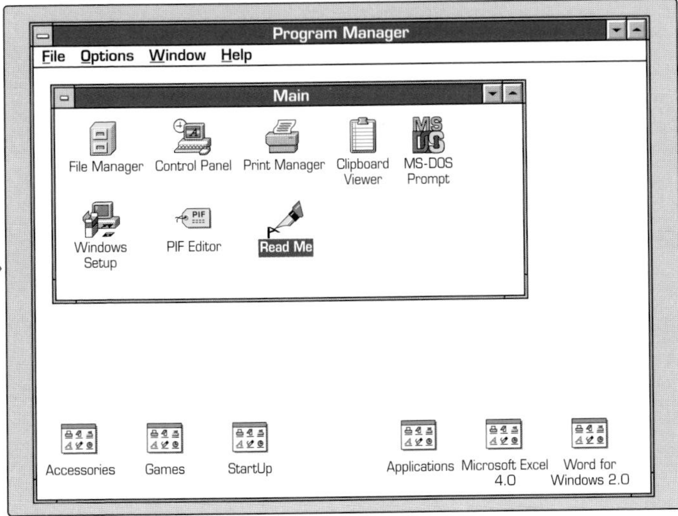

◆ When you exit Windows, the program will store the last arrangement of icons and windows on your screen.

◆ This arrangement will appear the next time you start Windows.

EXIT WINDOWS

Exit Windows

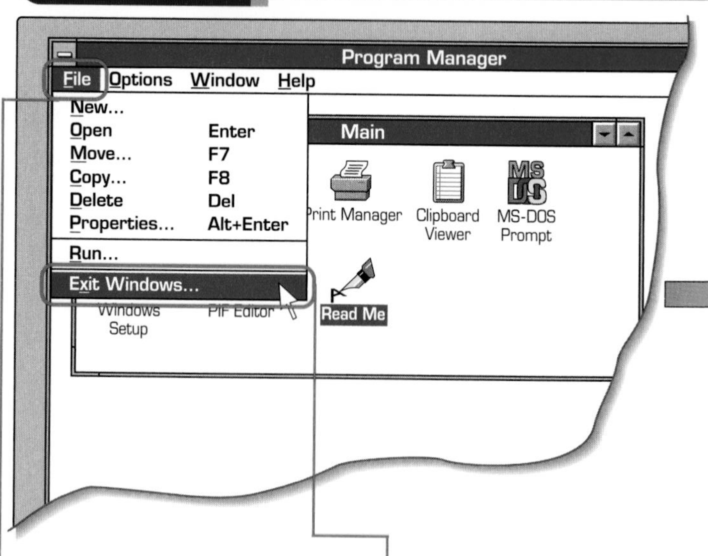

1 Move the mouse over **File** and then press the left button.

2 Move the mouse over **Exit Windows** and then press the left button.

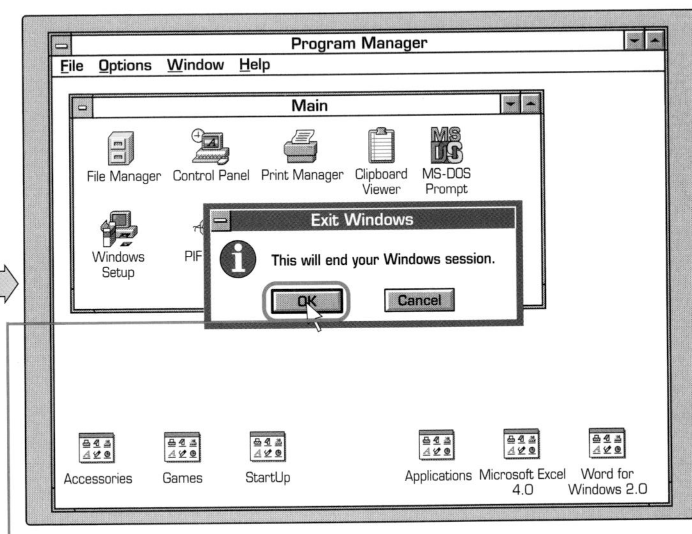

◆ The **Exit Windows** dialog box appears.

3 To exit Windows, move the mouse over **OK** and then press the left button.

◆ You are returned to the MS-DOS prompt (**C:**).

*Note: To return to Windows, type **WIN** and then press* **Enter**.

MOVE A WINDOW

Move a Window

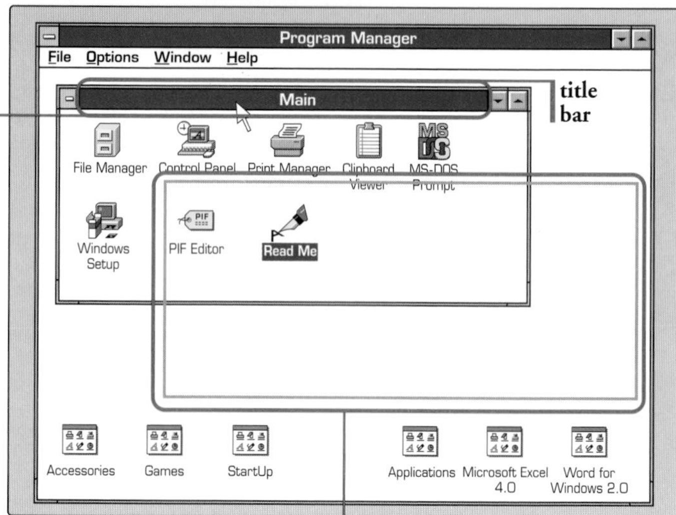

1 To move a window (example: **Main**), move the mouse over its title bar and then press and hold down the left button.

2 Still holding down the button, drag the window to a new location.

◆ A gray rectangle indicates the new location.

You can move a window from one location to another. This enables you to organize your desktop and display windows previously hidden from view.

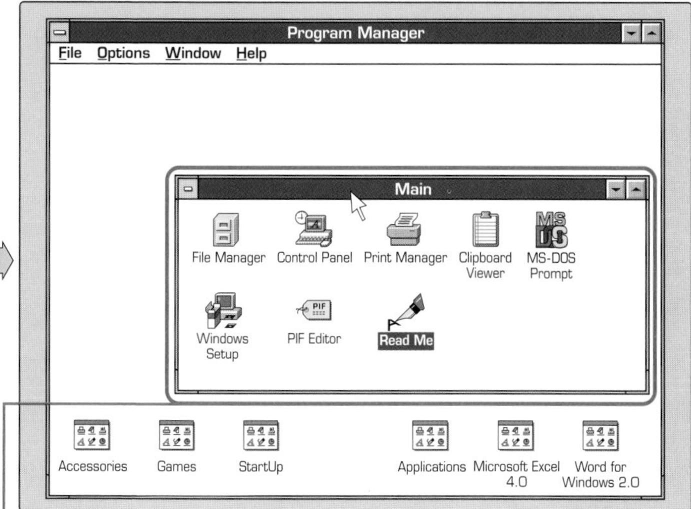

3 Release the button and the window jumps to the new position.

Note: To cancel the move, press **Esc** *before releasing the button in step* **3**.

Note: You cannot move a group window outside the ***Program Manager*** *window.*

SIZE A WINDOW

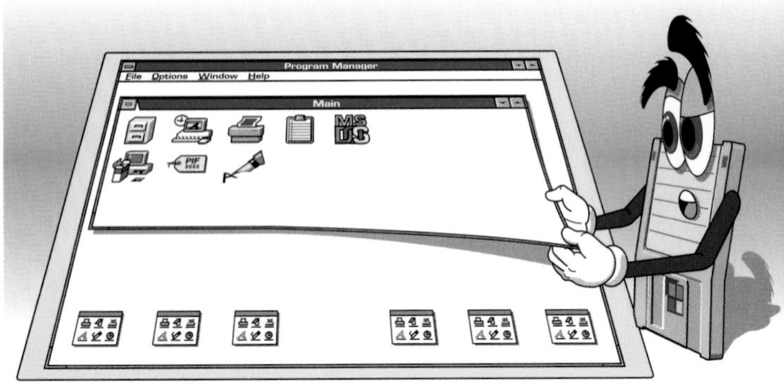

Size a Window

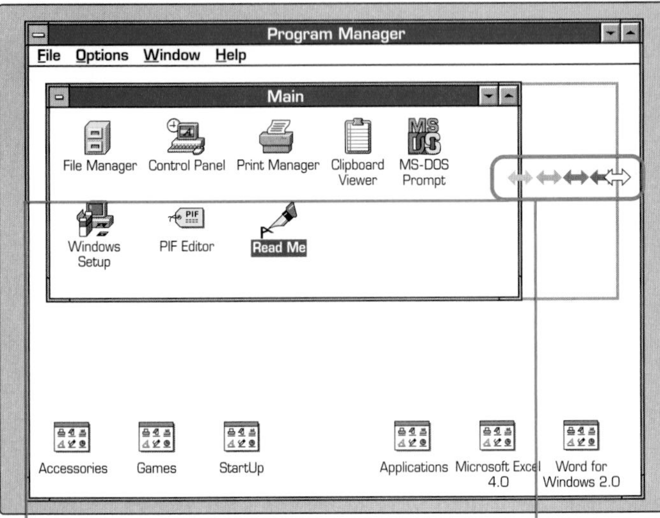

1 To change the size of a window, move the mouse over the right or left edge of the window (becomes ⇔).

2 Press and hold down the left button as you drag the edge of the window to the desired size.

◆ A gray outline indicates the new size.

You can change the size of any window on your screen. By increasing the size of a window, you can view icons that were previously hidden.

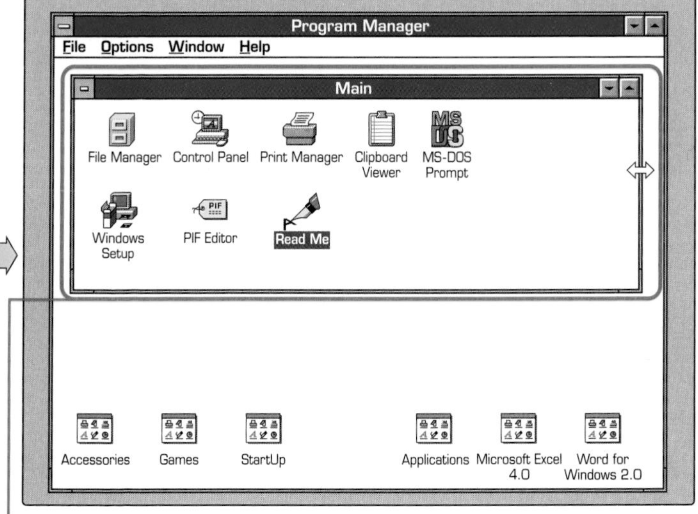

3 Release the button and the window is resized.

Note: To cancel the resizing, press **Esc** *before releasing the button in step* **3**.

◆ You can increase or decrease the size of a window from any edge or corner.

MOVE ICONS

Move Icons

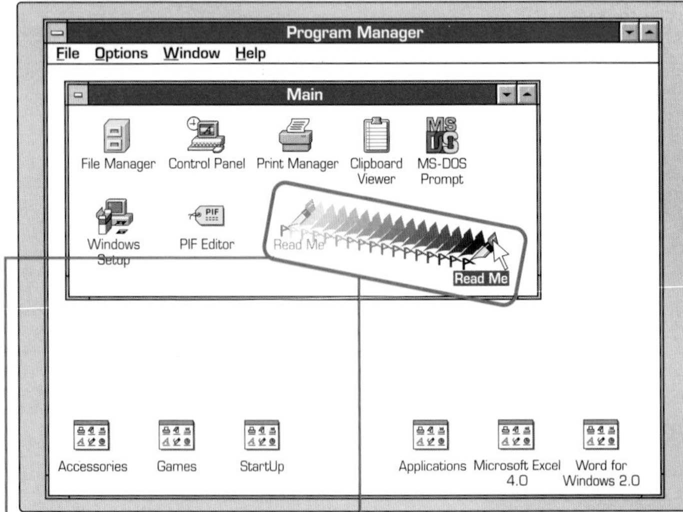

1 Move the mouse over the icon you want to move (example: **Read Me**).

2 Press and hold down the left button as you drag the icon to a new position in the window.

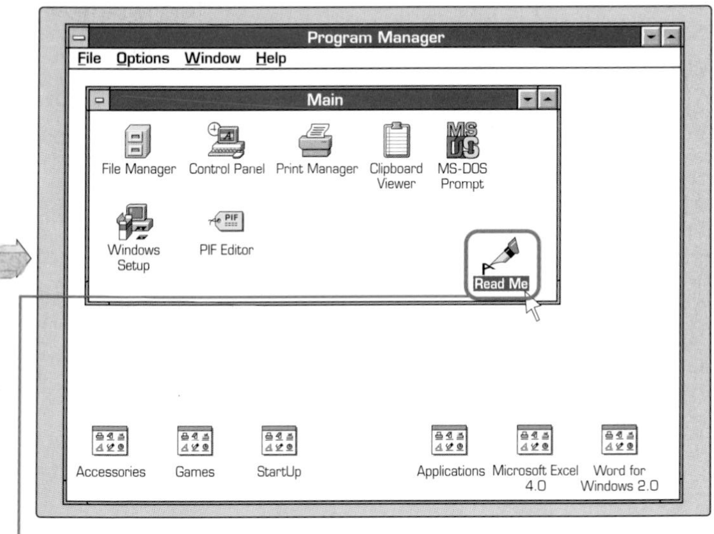

3 Release the button and the icon stays in the new position.

Note: You cannot move an icon if the ***Auto Arrange*** *command is* ***on****. For more information, refer to page 28.*

ARRANGE ICONS

Arrange Icons

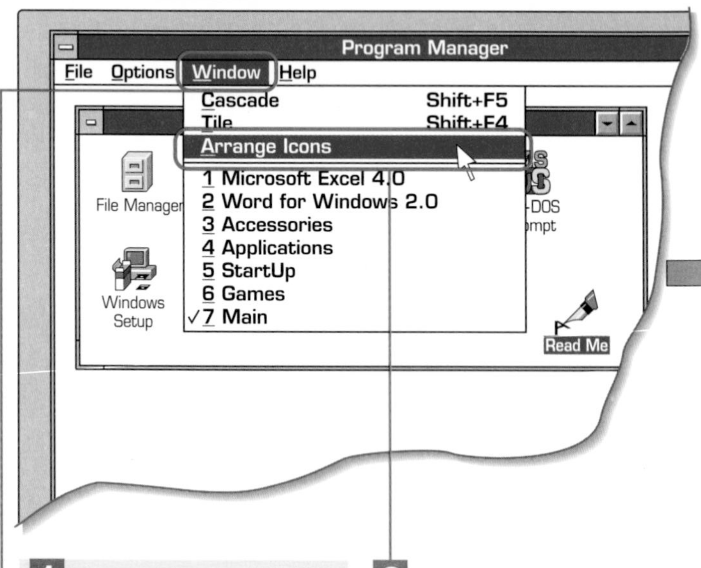

1 To quickly arrange all the icons in the active group window, move the mouse ⇖ over **Window** and then press the left button.

2 Move the mouse ⇖ over **Arrange Icons** and then press the left button.

To quickly arrange all the icons in the active group window, press Alt, W, A.

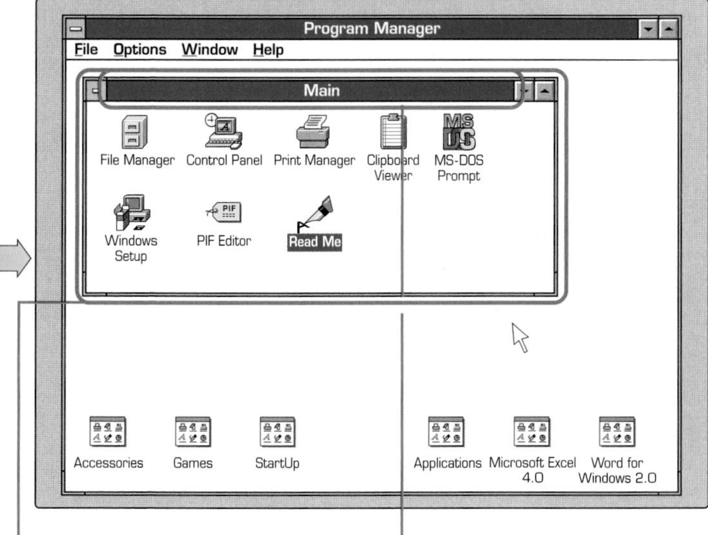

◆ The icons in the active group window are displayed in an orderly fashion.

◆ The active group window is identified by a blue title bar (example: **Main**).

Note: To make a window active, move the mouse anywhere over the window and then press the left button.

AUTO ARRANGE ICONS

If you change the size of a window and the Auto Arrange command is on, Windows will automatically rearrange the icons in that window for you.

Auto Arrange Icons

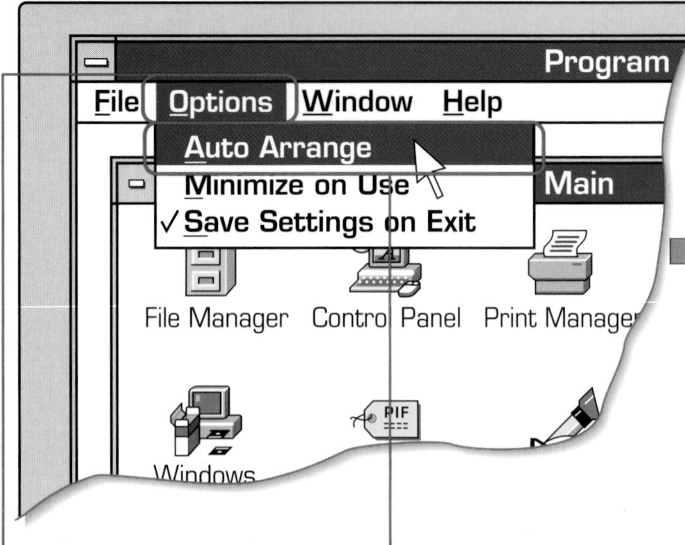

1 To turn the **Auto Arrange** command on, move the mouse ↖ over **Options** and then press the left button.

2 Move the mouse ↖ over **Auto Arrange** and then press the left button.

*Note: If a check mark (✓) appears beside **Auto Arrange**, the command is already on. To leave the command on, press* Alt.

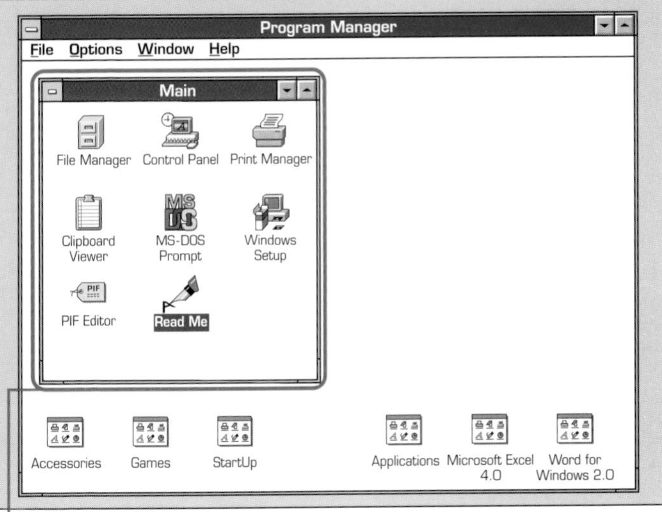

◆ If you change the size of a window, the icons automatically rearrange to fit neatly within the window.

Note: To change the size of a window, refer to page 22.

MINIMIZE A WINDOW

Minimize a Window

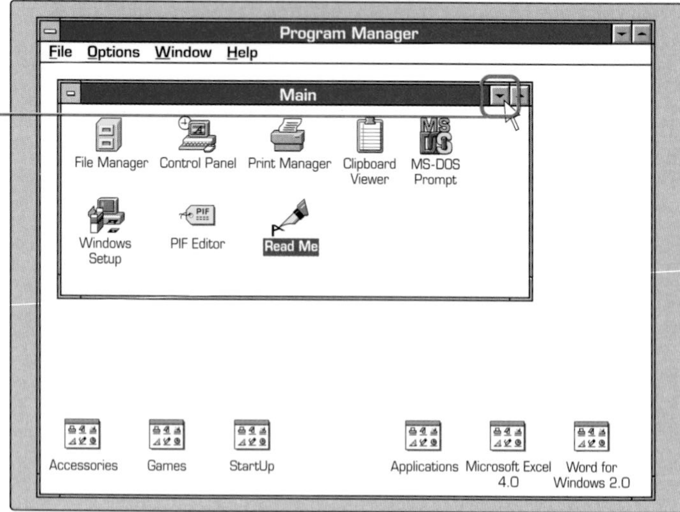

1 To reduce a window to an icon, move the mouse over its **Minimize** button and then press the left button.

When you finish working with a window, you can minimize (reduce) it to an icon. This provides you with more working space on your screen.

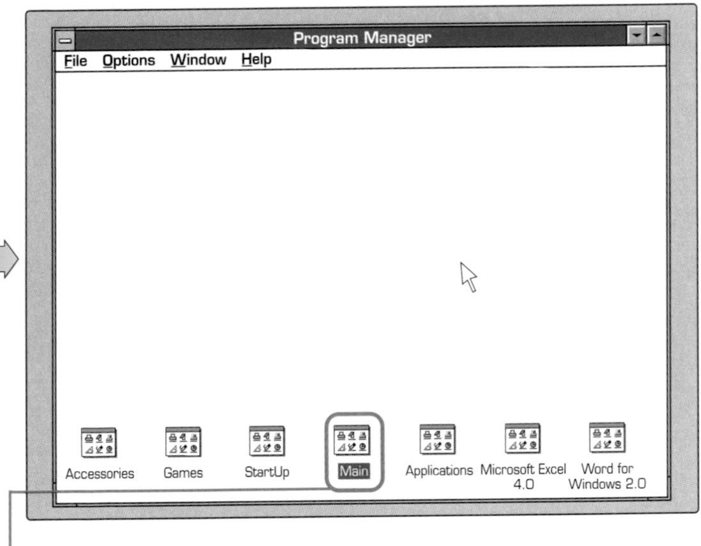

◆ The window is reduced to an icon.

RESTORE AN ICON

Restore an Icon

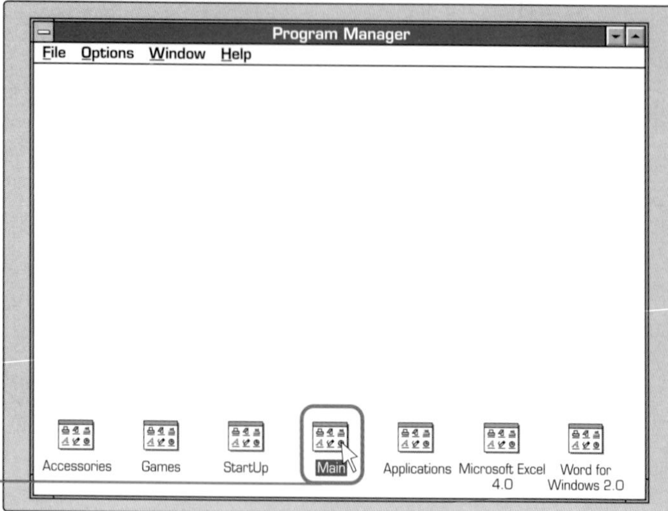

1 To restore an icon to a window, move the mouse over the icon (example: **Main**) and then quickly press the left button twice.

You can restore an icon to a window to display its contents. The window returns to its original size.

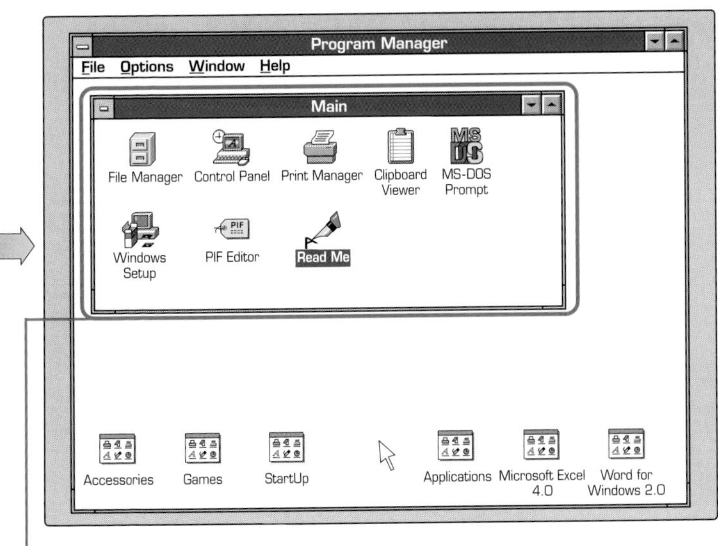

◆ The icon is restored to a window.

MAXIMIZE A WINDOW

You can enlarge a window to its maximum size. This enables you to view more of its contents.

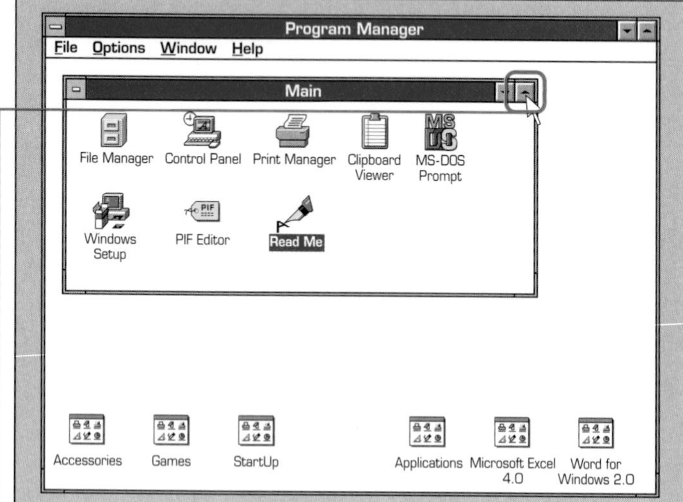

1 To enlarge a window (example: **Main**), move the mouse ⇖ over its **Maximize** button and then press the left button.

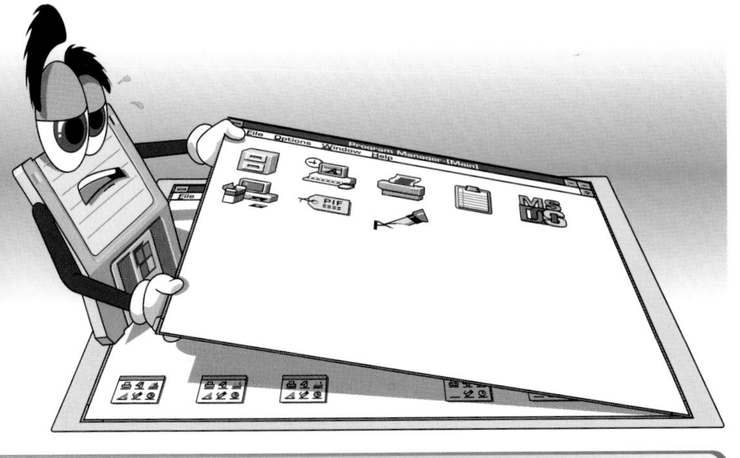

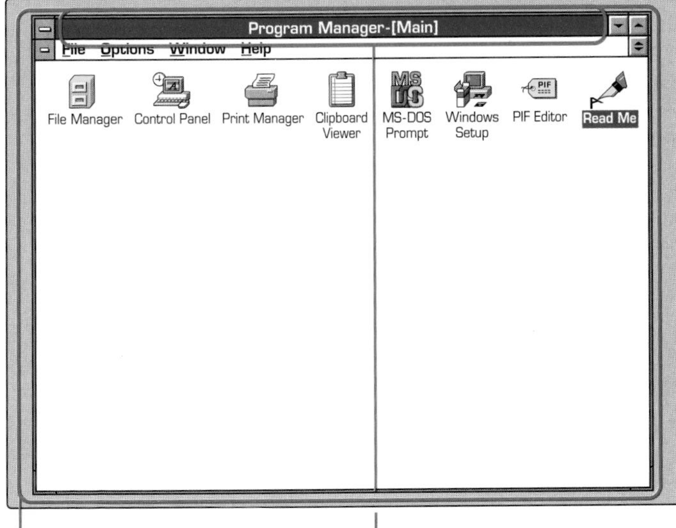

◆ The window enlarges to fill the entire area in the **Program Manager** window.

◆ The title bar is now shared. The name of the group window appears in square brackets (example: [**Main**]).

RESTORE A WINDOW

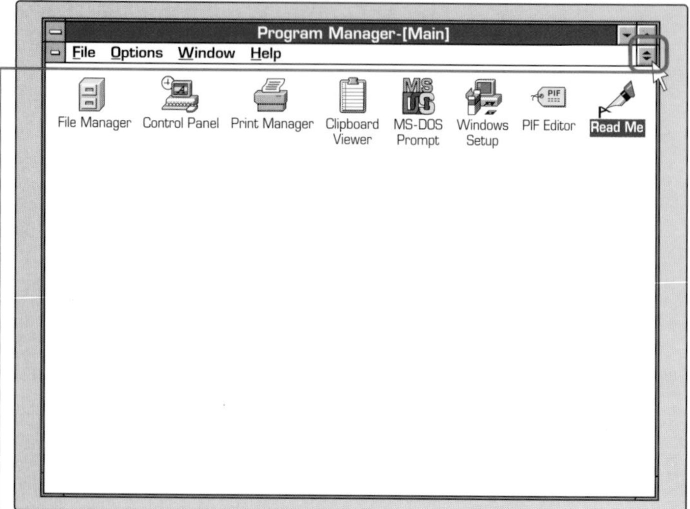

1 To restore a window (example: **Main**), move the mouse ⇖ over its **Restore** button and then press the left button.

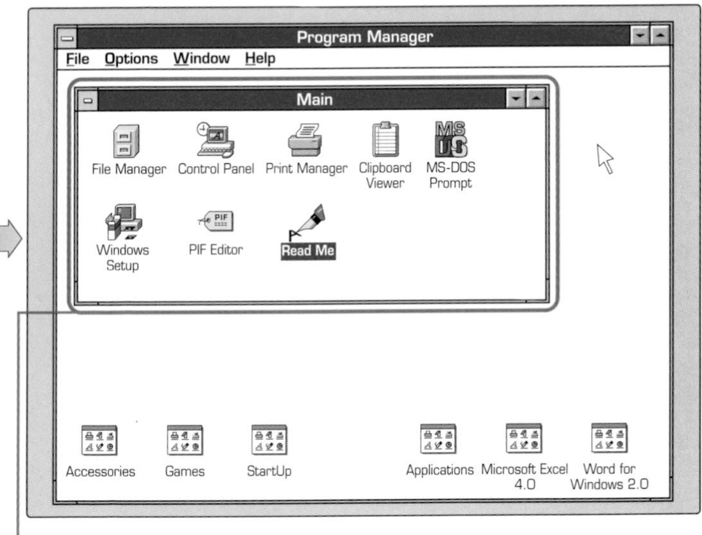

◆ The window is restored to its original size.

OPEN GROUP WINDOWS

◆ The first time you start Windows, the **Main** group window is open.

1 To open another group window (example: **Accessories**), move the mouse ⇖ over its icon and then quickly press the left button twice.

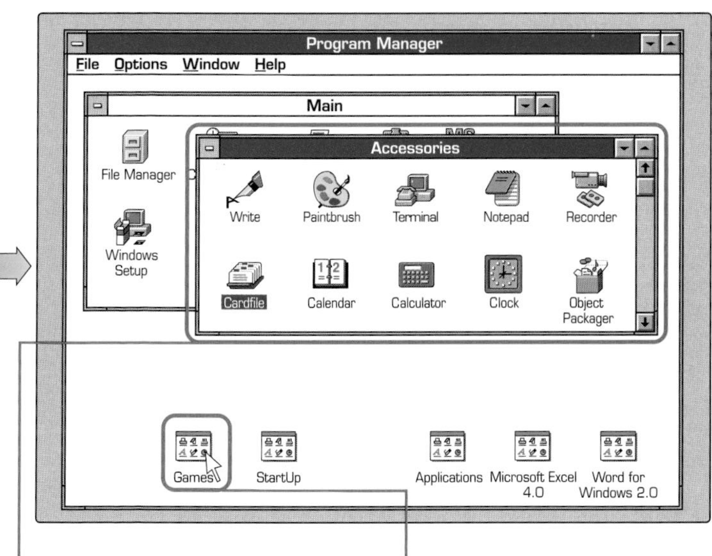

◆ The window opens and becomes the active window.

◆ You can only work with the active window, which displays a blue title bar.

2 To open another group window (example: **Games**), move the mouse ⇖ over its icon and then quickly press the left button twice.

SWITCH BETWEEN GROUP WINDOWS

Switch Between Group Windows

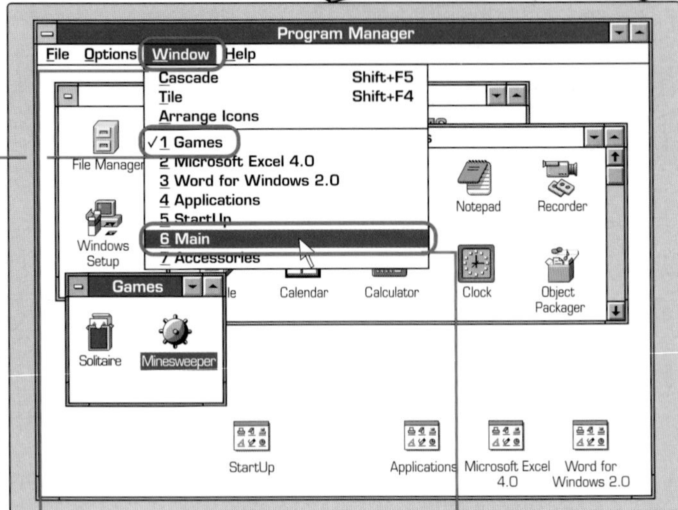

1 To switch to another group window, move the mouse ⇖ over **Window** and then press the left button.

◆ A check mark (✓) is displayed beside the name of the active group window (example: **Games**).

2 Move the mouse ⇖ over the name of the window you want to switch to (example: **Main**) and then press the left button.

Tip:

Think of each window as a separate piece of paper. When you open a window, you are placing a new piece of paper on your screen. Sometimes, the pieces of paper overlap.

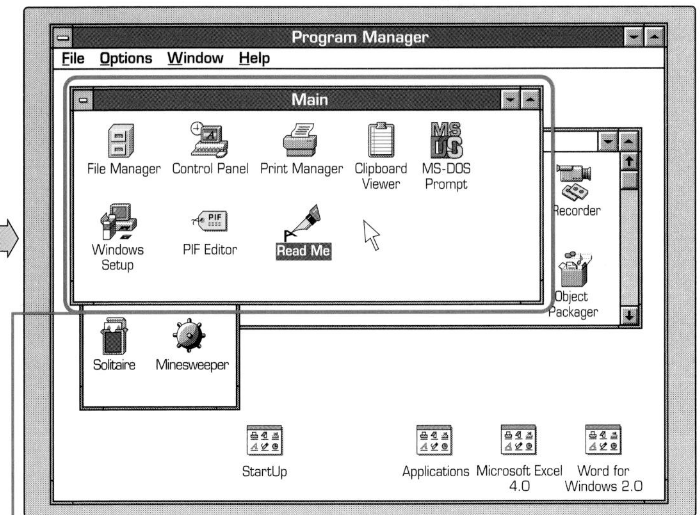

◆ The window you selected now becomes the active window (example: **Main**).

Note: This method is useful if the group window you want to view is completely covered by another window.

SHORTCUT

Move the mouse over the window you want to switch to and then press the left button.

CASCADE GROUP WINDOWS

Cascade Group Windows

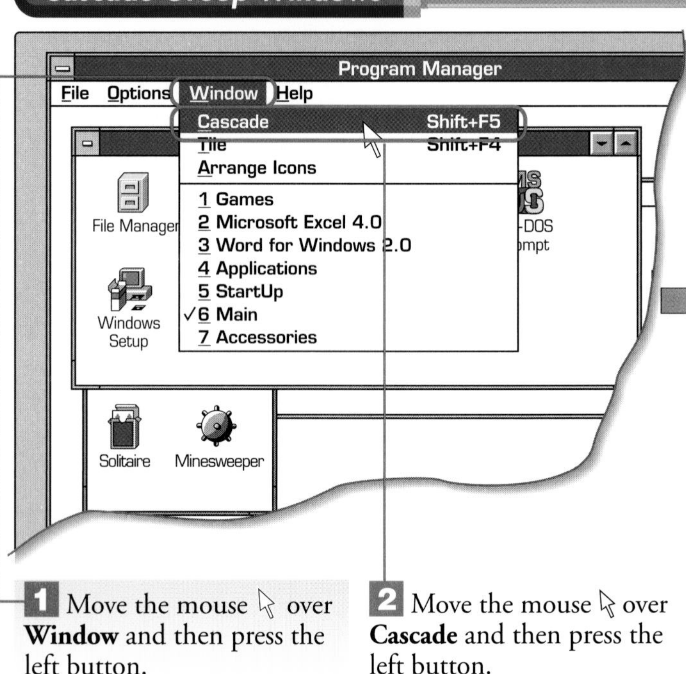

1 Move the mouse over **Window** and then press the left button.

2 Move the mouse over **Cascade** and then press the left button.

If you have several group windows open, some of them may be hidden from view. The Cascade command allows you to display all your open group windows by overlapping them.

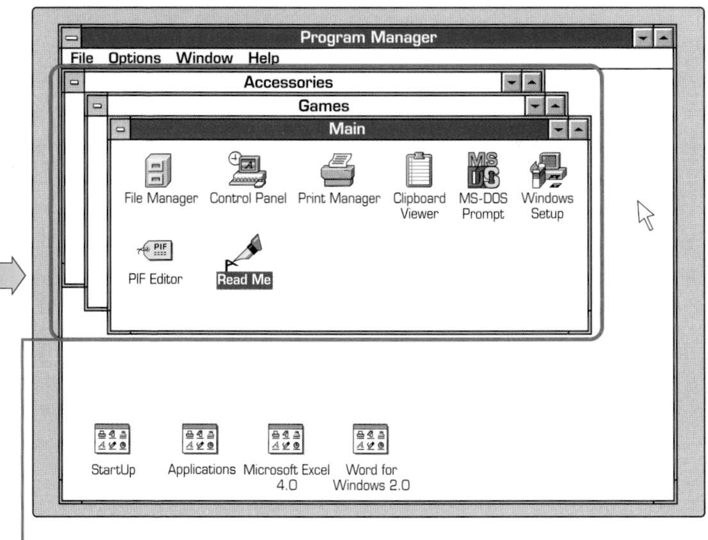

◆ The group windows are cascaded.

TILE GROUP WINDOWS

Tile Group Windows

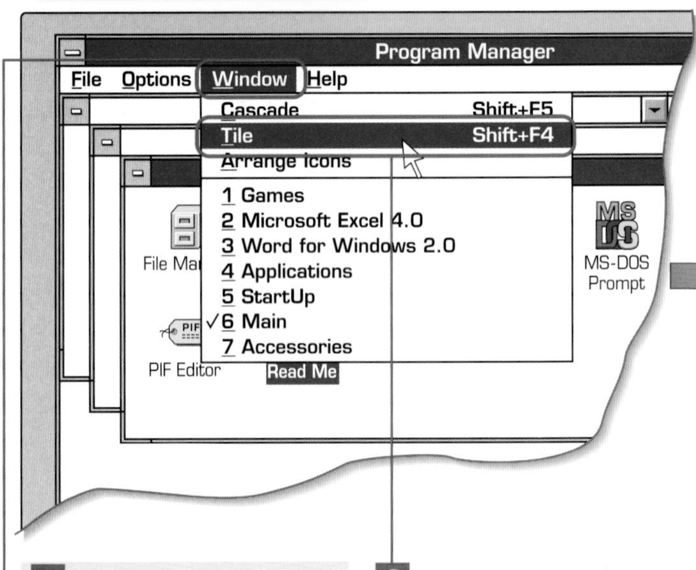

1 Move the mouse ↖ over **Window** and then press the left button.

2 Move the mouse ↖ over **Tile** and then press the left button.

The Tile command lets you display all your open group windows side-by-side without overlapping them. This enables you to view the contents of each window.

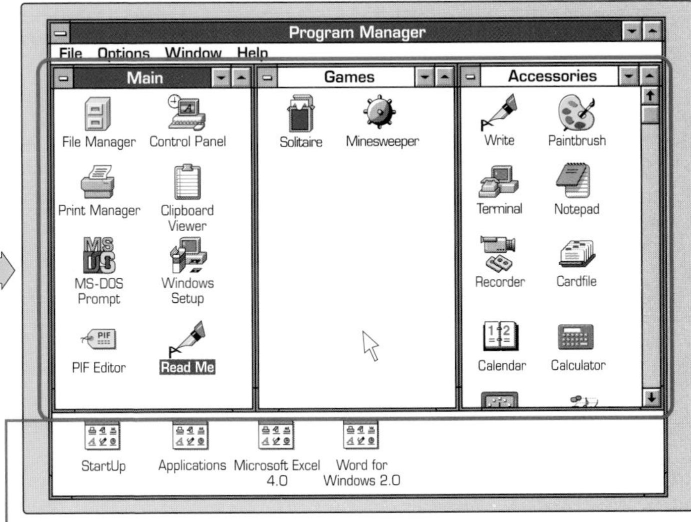

◆ The group windows are tiled.

SCROLL THROUGH A WINDOW

Scroll Down or Up One Line

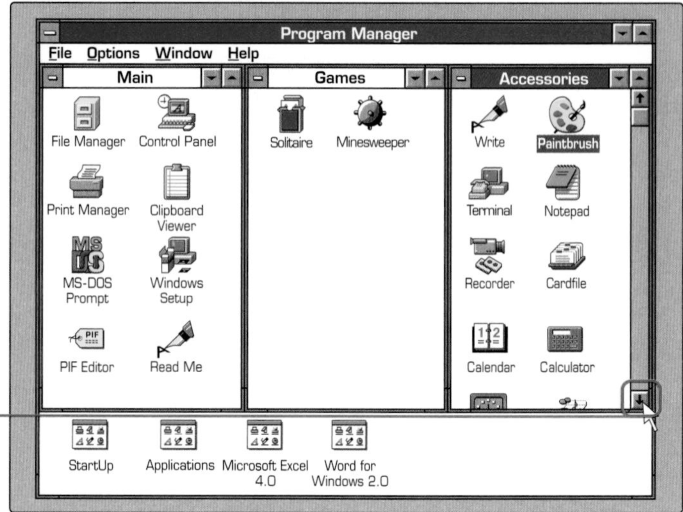

Scroll Down

1 Move the mouse over the down scroll arrow and then press the left button.

Scroll bars appear when a window is not large enough to display all of its icons. To view the rest of these "hidden" icons, you can scroll through the window.

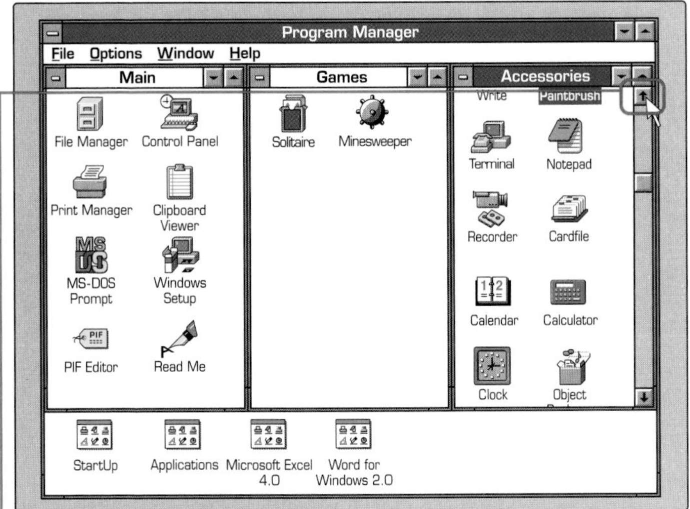

Scroll Up

1 Move the mouse over the up scroll arrow and then press the left button.

SCROLL THROUGH A WINDOW

Scroll Quickly Through a Window

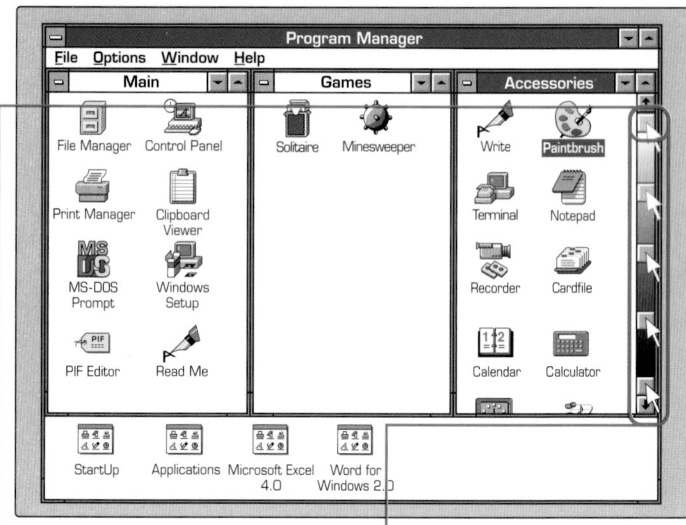

1 Move the mouse over the scroll box and then press and hold down the left button.

2 Still holding down the button, drag the scroll box straight down to the end of the scroll bar.

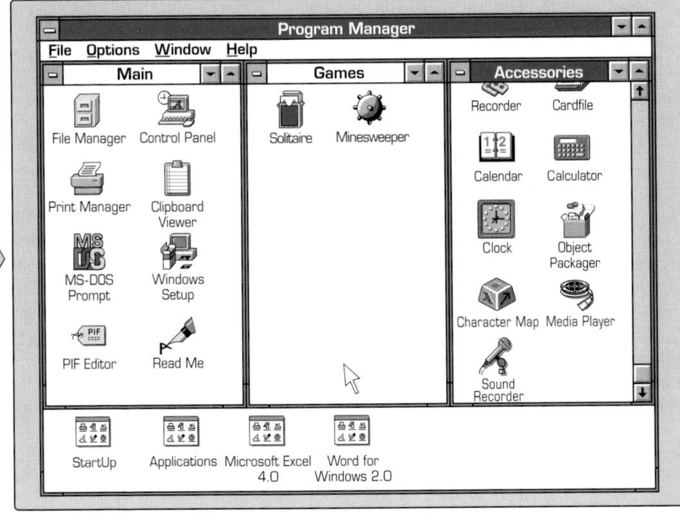

3 Release the button.

SEARCH FOR HELP

Search for Help

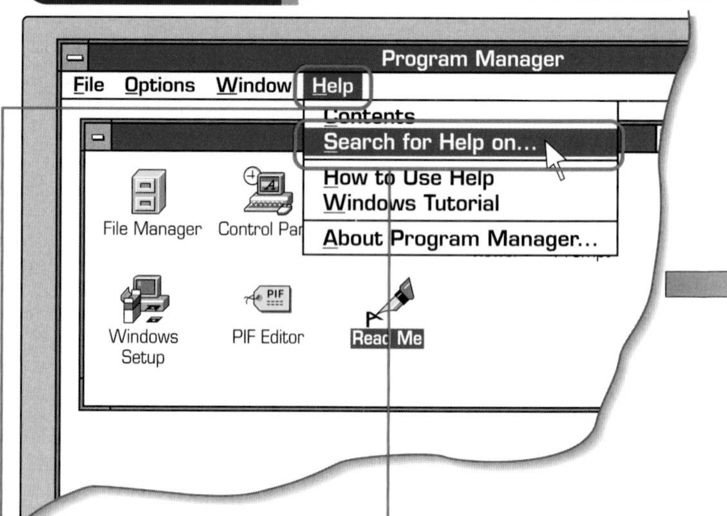

1 Move the mouse over **Help** and then press the left button.

2 Move the mouse over **Search for Help on** and then press the left button. The **Search** dialog box appears.

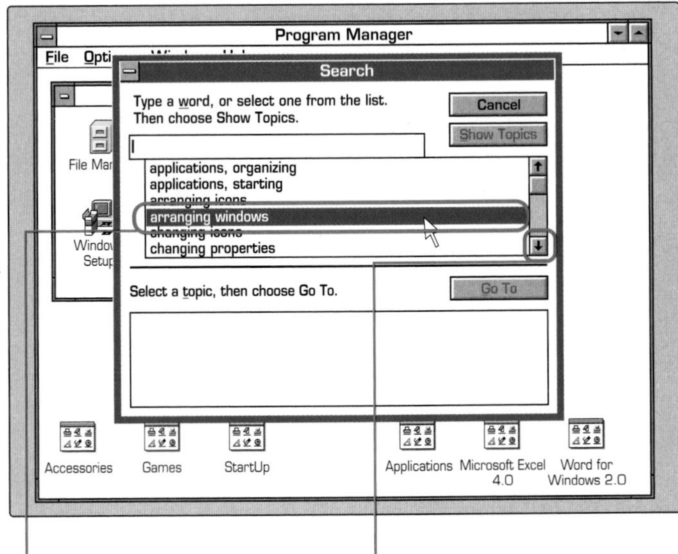

3 Move the mouse over the topic you want help on (example: **arranging windows**) and then quickly press the left button twice.

◆ To view more topics, move the mouse over the down scroll arrow and then press the left button.

Note: To continue, refer to the next page.

Search for Help (Continued)

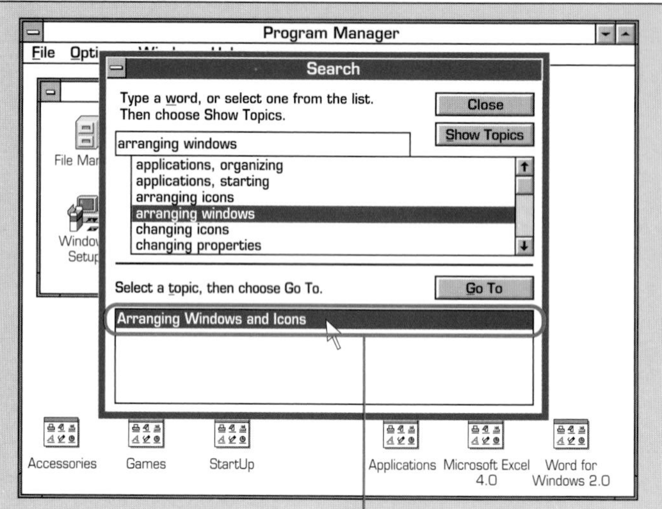

◆ A list of the available topics in the category appears.

Note: In this example, only one topic is displayed.

4 Move the mouse over the topic of interest (example: **Arranging Windows and Icons**) and then quickly press the left button twice.

Tip:

To print the help topic displayed on your screen:

1 Move the mouse over **File** and then press the left button.

2 Move the mouse over **Print Topic** and then press the left button.

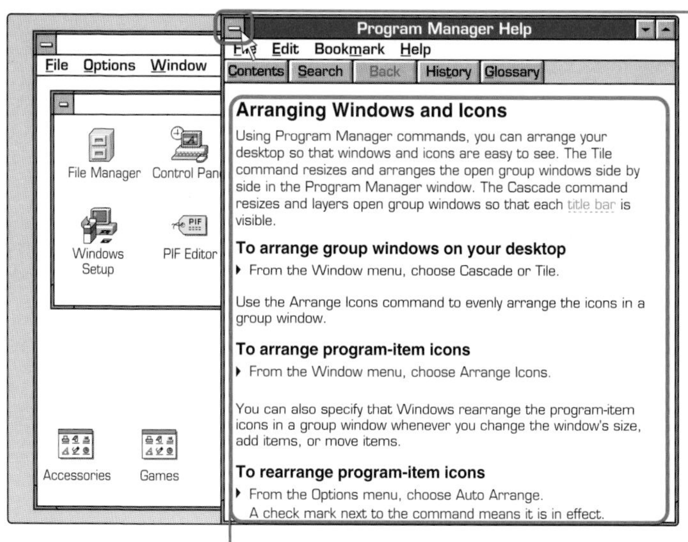

◆ Information on the selected topic appears.

*Note: You can also access the **Search** dialog box by moving the mouse over Search and then pressing the left button.*

5 To close **Program Manager Help**, move the mouse over its **control-menu box** and then quickly press the left button twice.

START APPLICATIONS

Applications enable you to perform many different tasks on your computer. They help you write letters, sort information, draw pictures and even play games.

Start Applications

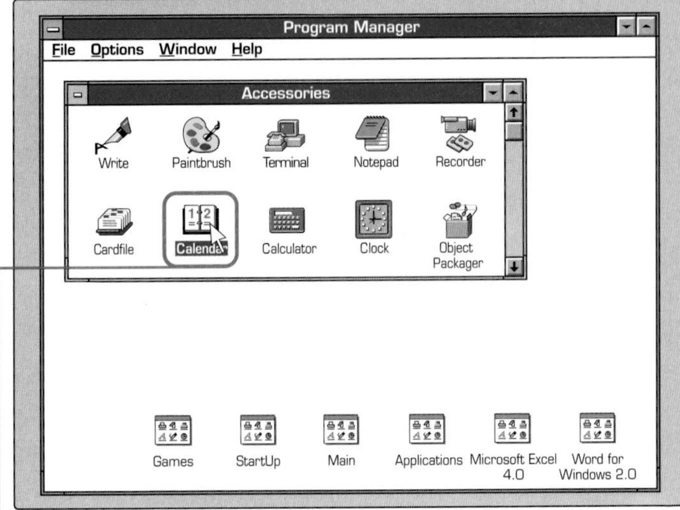

1 To start an application, move the mouse over its icon (example: **Calendar**) and then quickly press the left button twice.

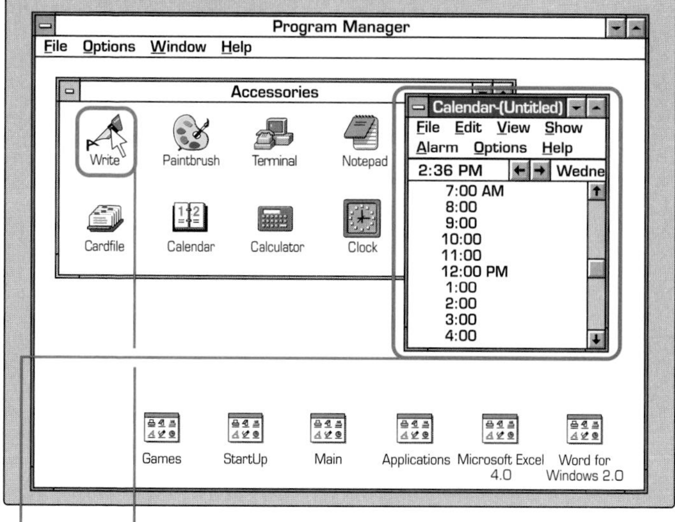

2 Size and move the window as shown above. This provides more room on your screen for any other applications you wish to start.

Note: To size a window, refer to page 22. To move a window, refer to page 20.

3 To start another application, move the mouse over its icon (example: **Write**) and then quickly press the left button twice.

Note: To continue, refer to the next page.

You can have several applications open at one time.

Start Applications (Continued)

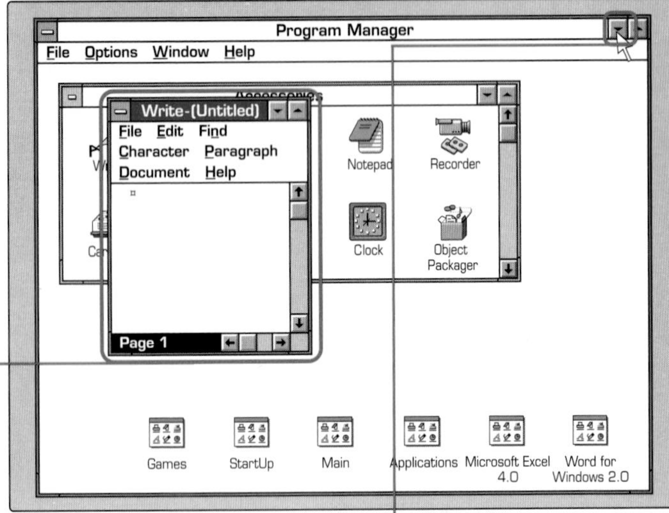

4 Size and move the window as shown above.

Note: Some open applications may become hidden behind the ***Program Manager*** *window (example:* ***Calendar****).*

5 To start another application (example: **Cardfile**), repeat steps **1** and **2** starting on page 54.

6 To reduce the **Program Manager** window to an icon, move the mouse over its **Minimize** button and then press the left button.

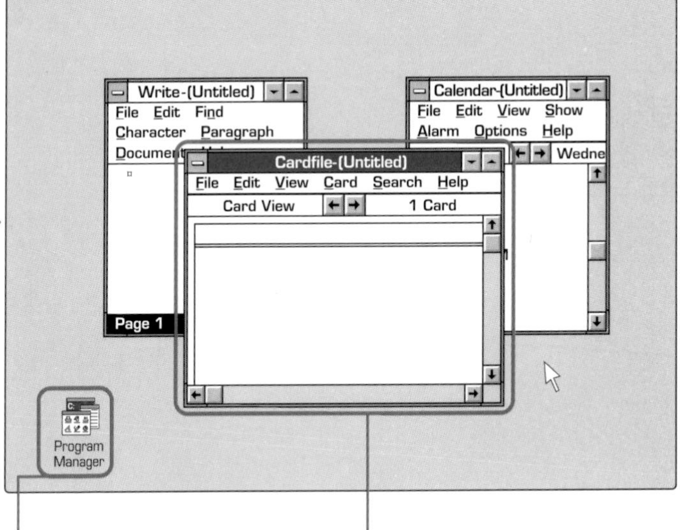

◆ The **Program Manager** is reduced to an icon. This clears your screen so you can view the other applications.

◆ The active application displays a blue title bar (example: **Cardfile**). You can only work with the active application.

SWITCH BETWEEN APPLICATIONS

Switch Between Applications (Method 1)

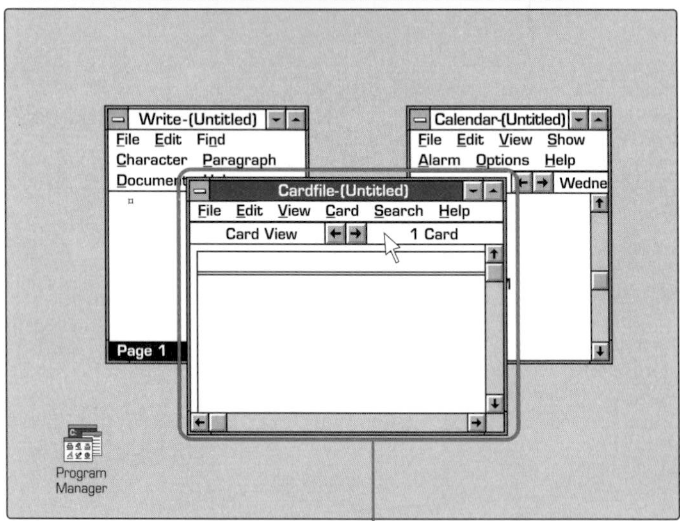

This method is useful if you only have a few applications open.

◆ The active application displays a blue title bar (example: **Cardfile**).

Note: You can only add or edit information in the active application.

If you have several applications open, some of them may be hidden. Switching between your applications enables you to view each one in turn.

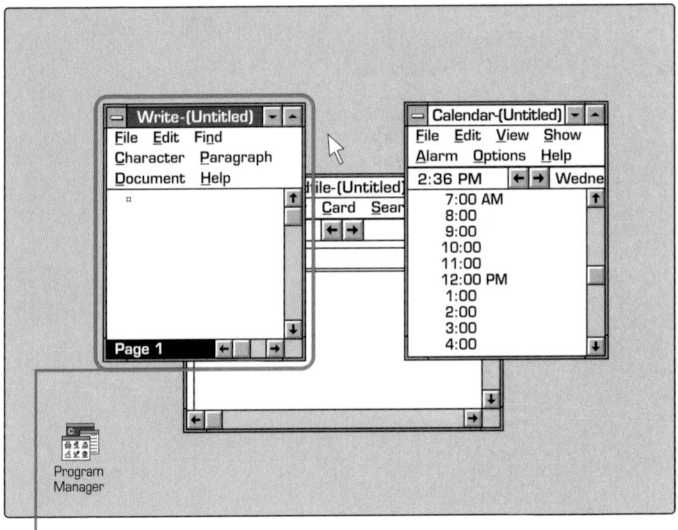

1 Press Alt + Esc until the application you want to switch to becomes active (example: **Write**).

SHORT CUT

To make an application active, move the mouse anywhere over its window and then press the left button.

SWITCH BETWEEN APPLICATIONS

Switch Between Applications (Method 2)

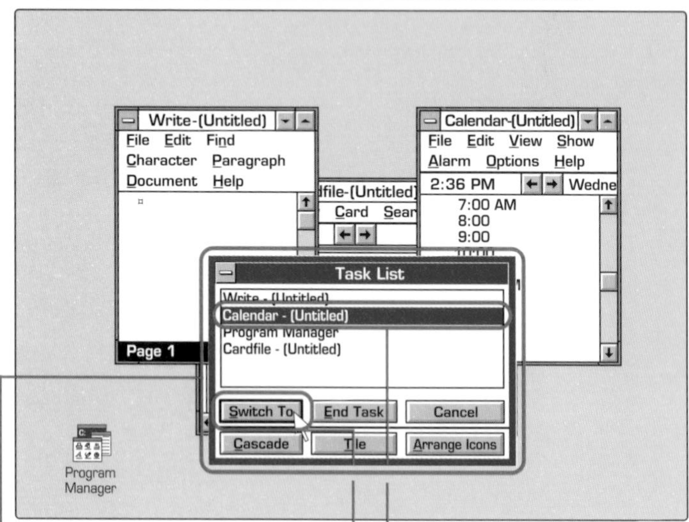

This method is useful if you have many applications open.

1 Press Ctrl + Esc and the **Task List** dialog box appears.

2 Move the mouse over the name of the application you want to switch to (example: **Calendar**) and then press the left button.

3 Move the mouse over **Switch To** and then press the left button.

You can use the Task List to switch between your open applications.

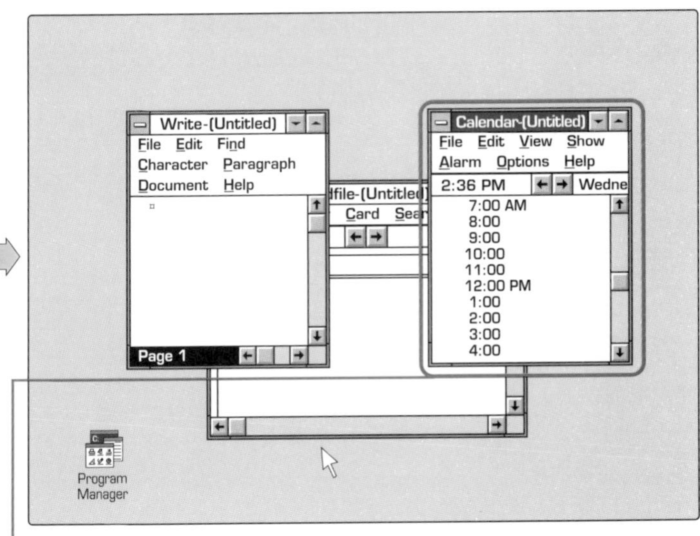

◆ The application window (example: **Calendar**) moves to the front and becomes the active window.

SHORTCUT

To display the **Task List** dialog box, move the mouse over any area on your screen not covered by a window and then quickly press the left button twice.

CASCADE APPLICATION WINDOWS

If you have several application windows open, some of them may be hidden from view. The Cascade command enables you to display all of your open application windows by overlapping them.

Cascade Application Windows

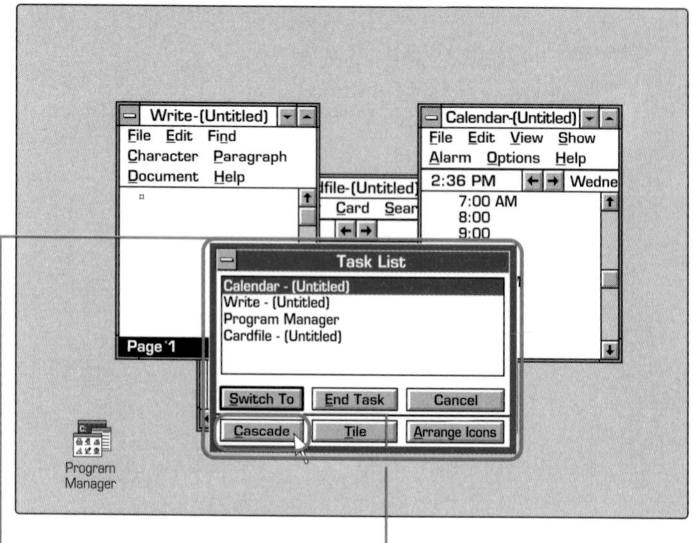

1 Press Ctrl + Esc and the **Task List** dialog box appears.

2 Move the mouse over **Cascade** and then press the left button.

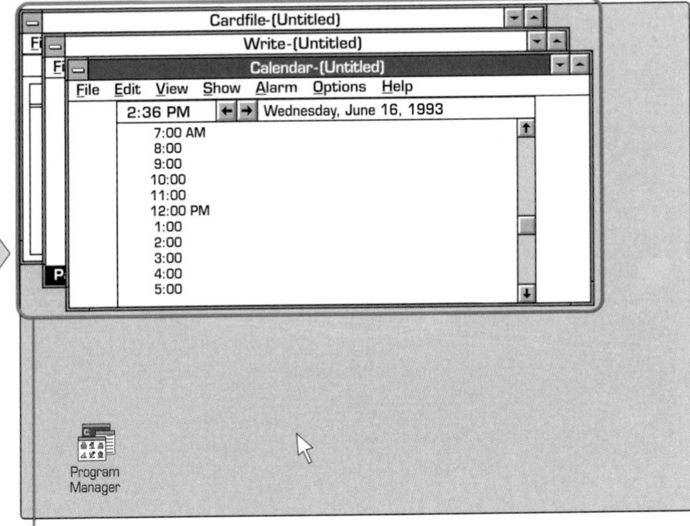

◆ The application windows are cascaded.

TILE APPLICATION WINDOWS

The Tile command lets you display all of your open application windows side-by-side without overlapping them. This enables you to view the contents of each window.

Tile Application Windows

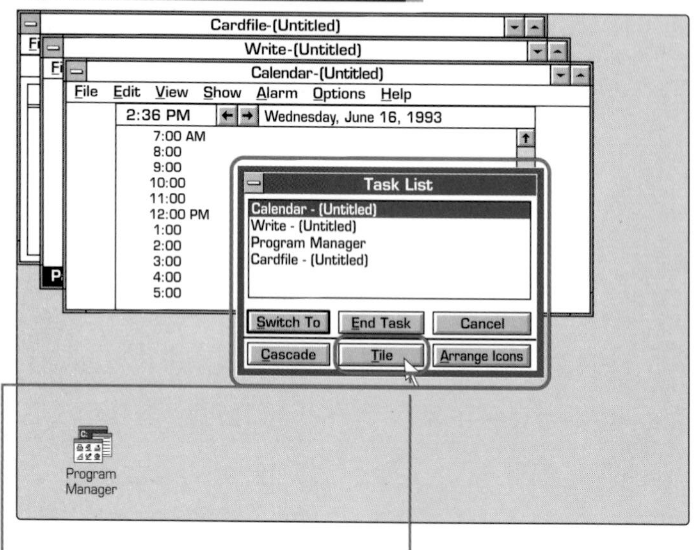

1 Press Ctrl + Esc and the **Task List** dialog box appears.

2 Move the mouse over **Tile** and then press the left button.

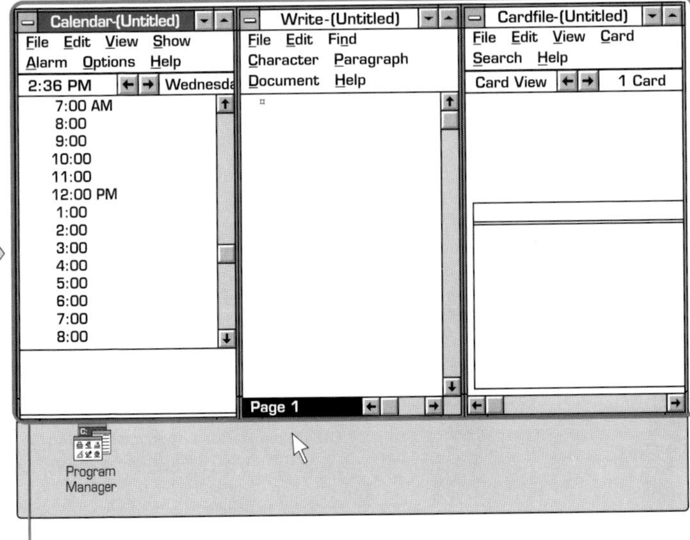

◆ The application windows are tiled.

ARRANGE APPLICATION ICONS

Arrange Application Icons

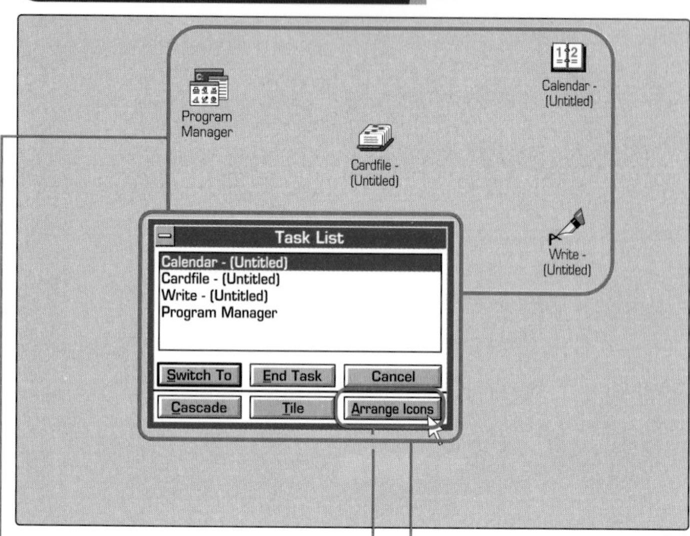

◆ In this example, reduce the applications to icons and then move them as shown above.

Note: To reduce an application to an icon, refer to page 30. To move an icon, refer to page 24.

1 Press Ctrl + Esc and the **Task List** dialog box appears.

2 Move the mouse over **Arrange Icons** and then press the left button.

If your application icons are scattered around your screen, you can use the Arrange Icons feature to line them up in an orderly fashion.

◆ The application icons are neatly arranged along the bottom of your screen.

Note: To restore an application to a window, move the mouse over its icon and then quickly press the left button twice.

CLOSE AN APPLICATION

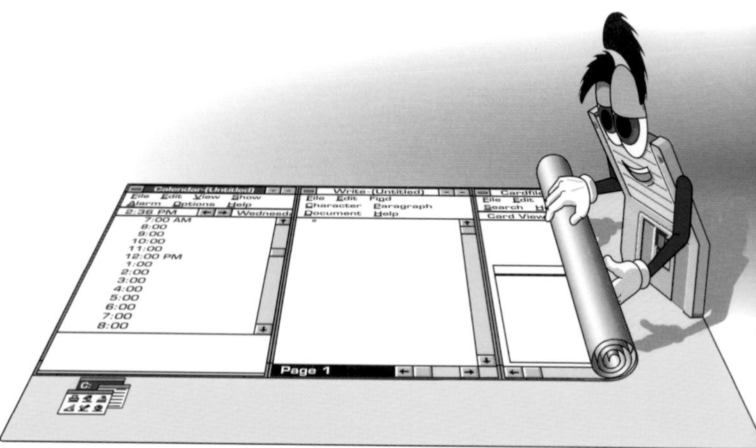

Close an Application

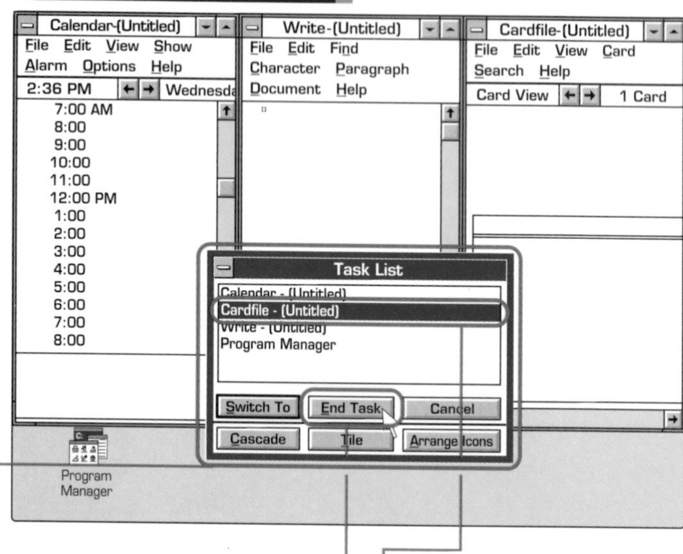

1 Press Ctrl + Esc and the **Task List** dialog box appears.

2 Move the mouse over the name of the application you want to close (example: **Cardfile**) and then press the left button.

3 Move the mouse over **End Task** and then press the left button.

Closing an application tells Windows you have completed a task. This will make room for other applications you want to use.

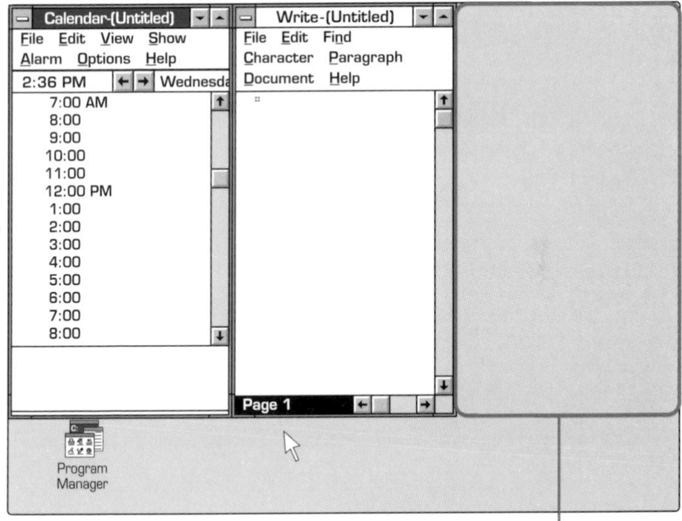

◆ The application closes and disappears from your screen.

SHORTCUT

To close an application, move the mouse over its **control-menu box** and then quickly press the left button twice.

DRIVES

Drives

◆ Most computers have one hard drive and one or two floppy drives. The hard drive is called drive **C**. The floppy drives are called drives **A** and **B**.

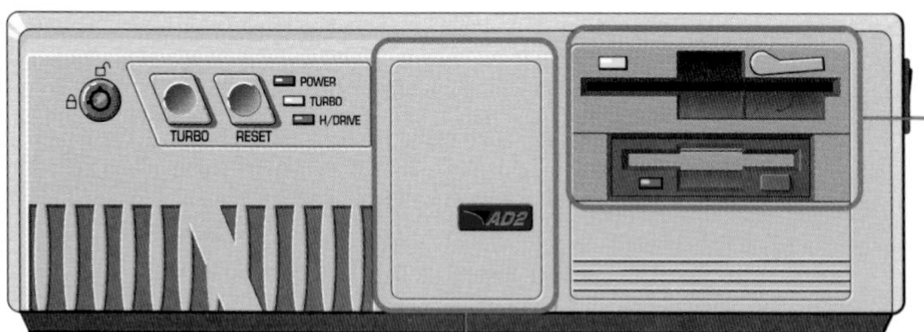

Hard drive (C:)

◆ A hard drive permanently stores programs and data. Most computers have at least one hard drive, called drive **C**.

Note: Your computer may be set up to have additional hard drives (example: ***drive D****).*

DRIVE NAME

A: ◆ A drive name consists of two parts: the letter and a colon (:). The colon represents the word "drive." For example, **A:** refers to the **A drive**.

Floppy drives (A: and B:)

◆ A floppy drive stores programs and data on removable diskettes (or floppy disks). A diskette operates slower and stores less data than a hard drive.

Diskettes are used to:

- Load new programs.
- Store backup copies of data.
- Transfer data to other computers.

If your computer has only one floppy drive, it is called drive **A**.

If your computer has two floppy drives, the second drive is called drive **B**.

DIRECTORIES

Directories

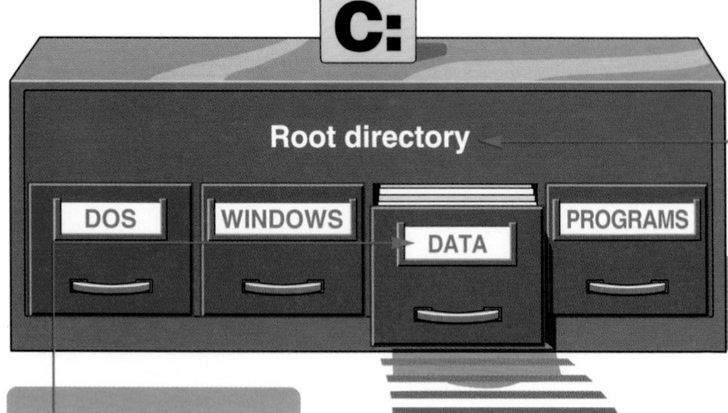

Directories

A directory usually contains related information. For example, the **DATA** directory contains all your data files.

Directories are like the drawers and folders in a filing cabinet. They help you organize the programs and data stored in the drives.

Root Directory

The main directory is called the root directory. All other directories are located below this directory.

Note: The \ symbol by itself stands for the root directory.

Files

A file is a document you name and save. It is stored in a directory.

PATH

If you require a file that is not stored in the default or standard directory, you must tell Windows where it is. A "path" is the direction you tell Windows to follow to locate that file.
C:
WPDATA
MERGE.LET
DOS
EXLDATA

IN EVERYDAY LANGUAGE

To locate the MERGE.LET file, you must:

Find the cabinet labeled **C:** and then

Go to the drawer labeled **DATA** and then

Go to the folder labeled **WPDATA** and then

Go to the file labeled **MERGE.LET**

**Go to equals **

IN COMPUTER LANGUAGE

To retrieve the MERGE.LET file, replace the words Go to with \\. Type the following:

C:\DATA\WPDATA\MERGE.LET

OPEN THE FILE MANAGER

Open the File Manager

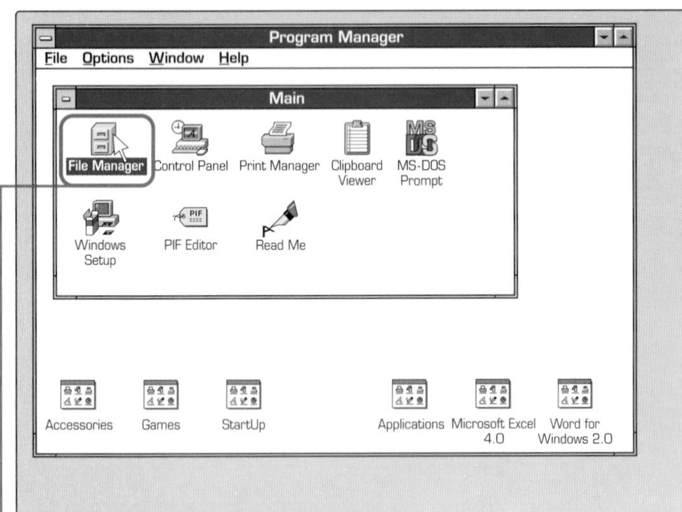

1 To open the **File Manager**, move the mouse over its icon and then quickly press the left button twice.

Windows includes a powerful program called the File Manager. This program functions like an electronic office, providing ways to organize and manage documents stored on your computer.

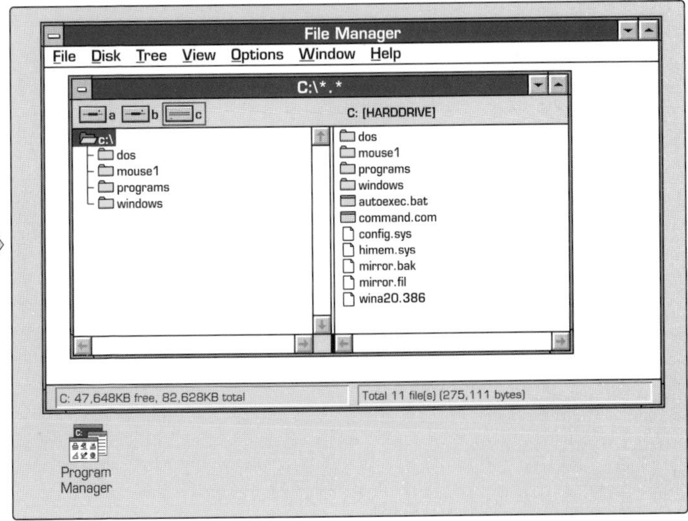

◆ The **File Manager** window appears.

*Note: To reduce the **Program Manager** window to an icon, move the mouse over its **Minimize** button and then press the left button.*

THE FILE MANAGER

The File Manager uses pictures (or icons) to represent the drives and directories on your computer.

The File Manager

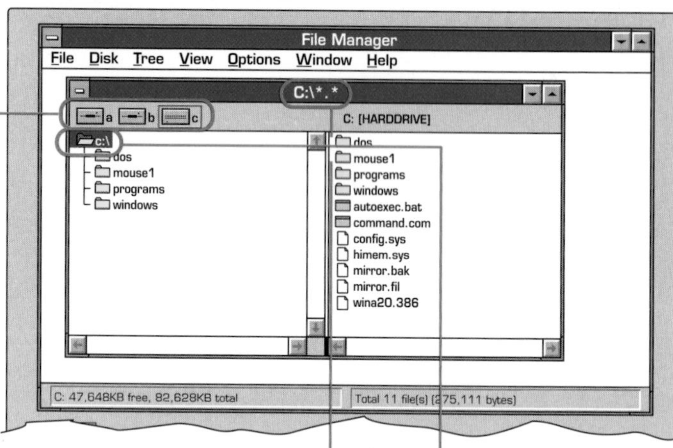

Drive Icons

Windows represents each floppy and hard drive on your computer as an icon and drive letter. The outlined icon is the current drive (example: **drive c**).

Current Directory

Windows highlights the current directory and displays it as an open folder.

Directory Path

The directory path displays the location of the current directory.

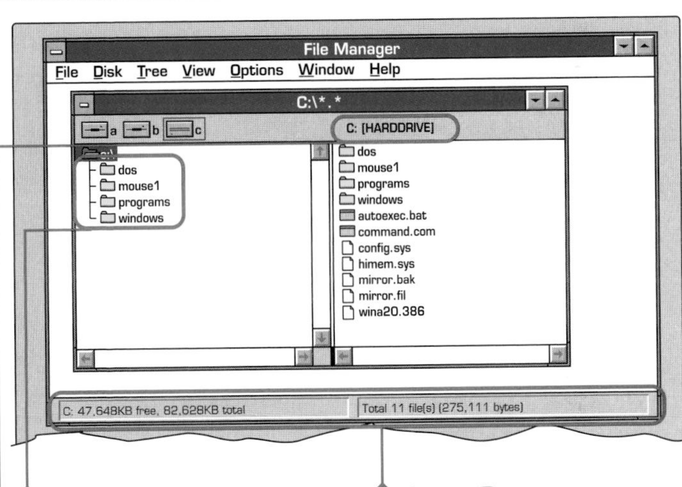

Directory Icons

Windows represents each directory as a folder. The directory folders are sorted in alphabetical order.

Volume Label

You can assign a name to each drive on your computer. The volume label name appears within the [ ] brackets (example: **HARDDRIVE**). Naming the drives is optional.

Status Bar

The status bar displays information about the current drive and the current directory.

CHANGE THE SCREEN FONT

Change the Screen Font

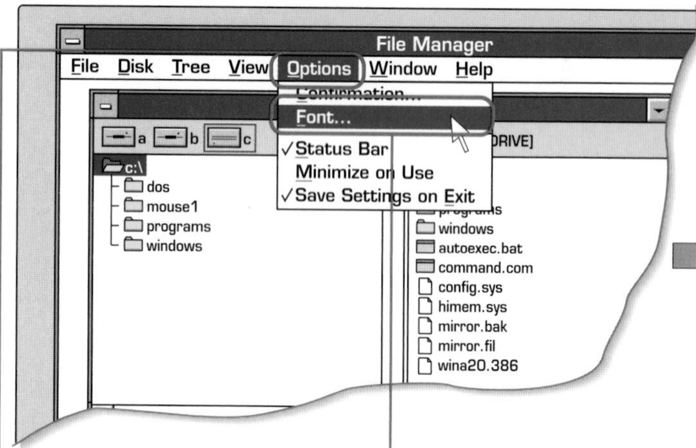

1 Move the mouse ↖ over **Options** and then press the left button.

Note: To open the ***File Manager****, refer to page 76.*

2 Move the mouse ↖ over **Font** and then press the left button.

◆ The **Font** dialog box appears.

A font refers to the design and size of the characters on your screen. You can change the screen font to suit your needs. For example, if the text is too small, you can increase its size.

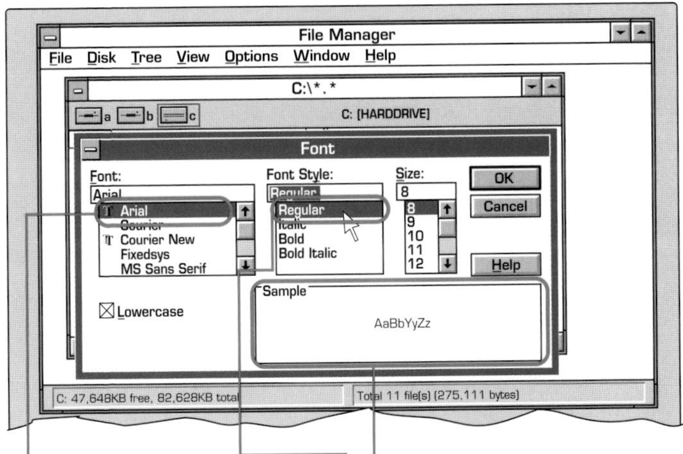

3 Move the mouse over the font you want to use (example: **Arial**) and then press the left button.

Note: To view more fonts, move the mouse over the up or down scroll arrow and then press the left button.

◆ A sample of the font appears. The sample changes as you select different font options.

4 Move the mouse over the font style you want to use (example: **Regular**) and then press the left button.

Note: To continue, refer to the next page.

CHANGE THE SCREEN FONT

Change the Screen Font (Continued)

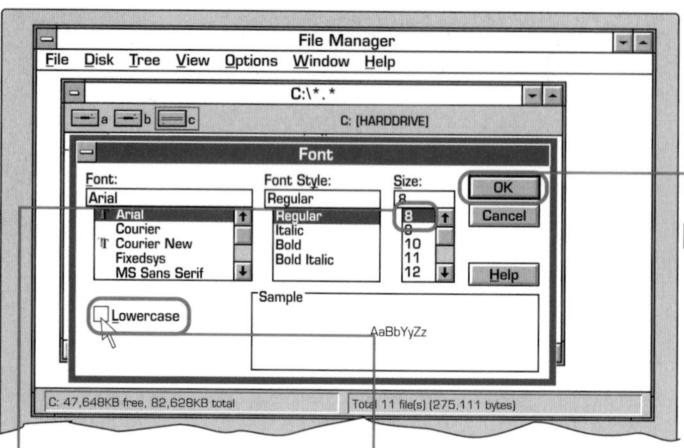

5 Move the mouse over the font size you want to use (example: **8**) and then press the left button.

Note: To view more sizes, move the mouse over the up or down scroll arrow and then press the left button.

6 To display the text in uppercase characters, move the mouse over the box beside **Lowercase** and then press the left button (☒ becomes ☐).

Note: To display the text in lowercase characters, repeat step **6** *(☐ becomes ☒).*

Windows offers many different font sizes and styles.

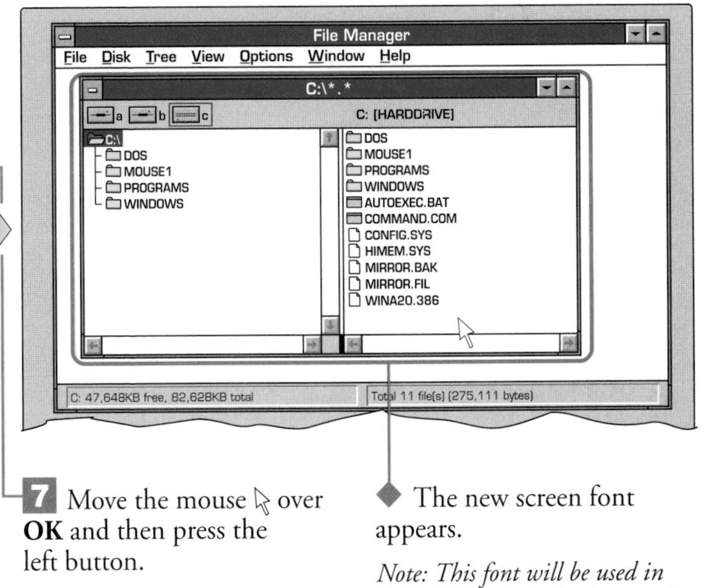

7 Move the mouse over **OK** and then press the left button.

◆ The new screen font appears.

Note: This font will be used in the ***File Manager*** *for the rest of this guide.*

CHANGE DRIVES

A B C Change Drives

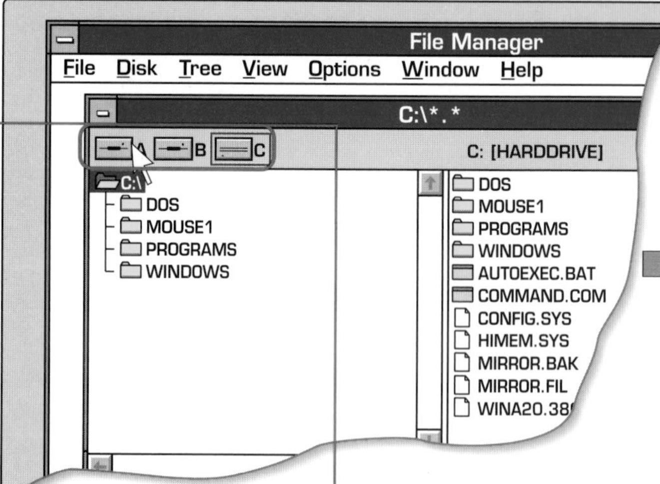

◆ Windows represents each floppy and hard drive on your computer as an icon and drive letter.

*Note: To open the **File Manager**, refer to page 76.*

◆ The current drive displays a border (example: **drive C**).

1 To change to another drive, move the mouse over its icon (example: **drive A**) and then press the left button.

Important!

If you want to change to a floppy drive, make sure you first insert a diskette into the drive.

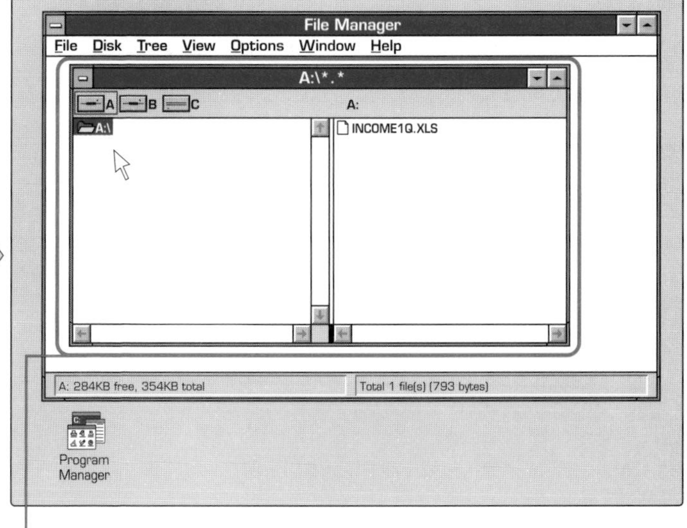

◆ The contents of the drive appear on your screen.

Note: To again display the contents of drive C, move the mouse over its icon (C) and then press the left button.

CHANGE DIRECTORIES

Change Directories

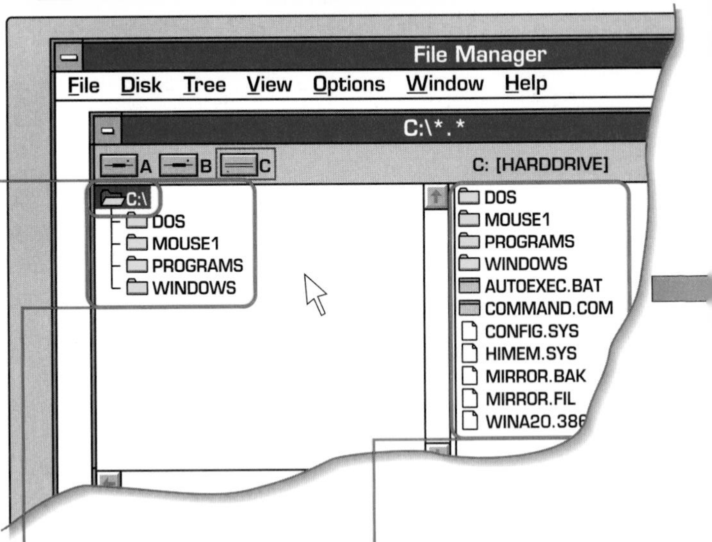

File Manager
File Disk Tree View Options Window Help
C:*.*
A B C
C: [HARDDRIVE]
C:\
DOS
MOUSE1
PROGRAMS
WINDOWS

DOS
MOUSE1
PROGRAMS
WINDOWS
AUTOEXEC.BAT
COMMAND.COM
CONFIG.SYS
HIMEM.SYS
MIRROR.BAK
MIRROR.FIL
WINA20.386

◆ Each folder represents a directory on your hard drive.

◆ Windows highlights the current directory and displays it as an open folder (example: **C:**).

◆ The subdirectories and files in the current directory are displayed.

*Note: To open the **File Manager**, refer to page 76.*

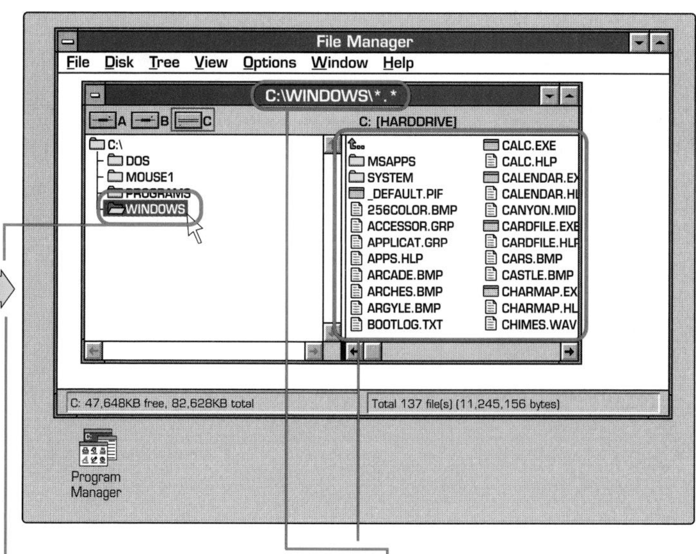

1 To change to another directory, move the mouse over its folder (example: **WINDOWS**) and then press the left button.

◆ The new current directory is highlighted.

◆ The location of the current directory is displayed at the top of your screen (example: **C:\WINDOWS**).

◆ The subdirectories and files in the current directory appear.

INDICATE EXPANDABLE BRANCHES

You can quickly see if your directories contain subdirectories by using the Indicate Expandable Branches command.

Indicate Expandable Branches

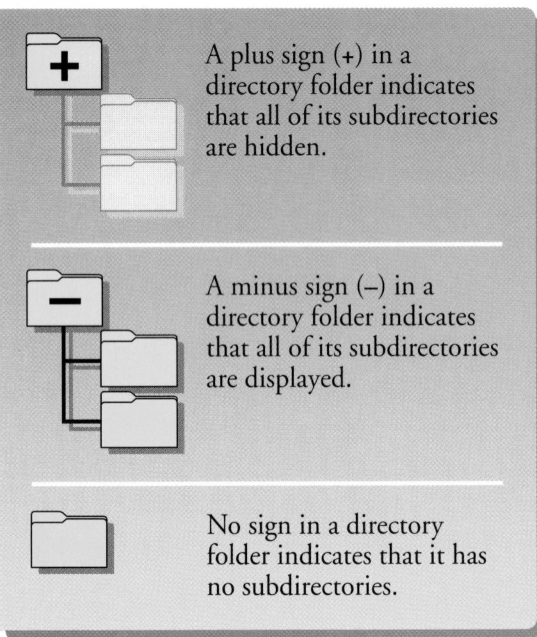

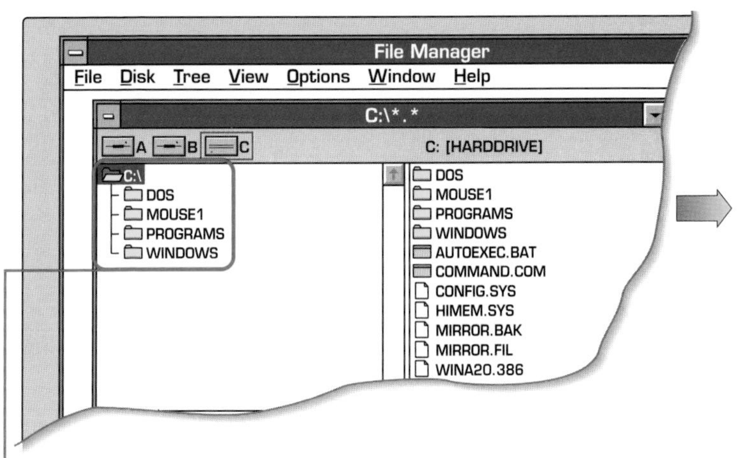

◆ When the **Indicate Expandable Branches** command is **off**, plus (+) and minus (–) signs are not displayed in the directory folders.

*Note: To open the **File Manager**, refer to page 76.*

Note: To turn on the command, refer to the next page.

INDICATE EXPANDABLE BRANCHES

Indicate Expandable Branches (Continued)

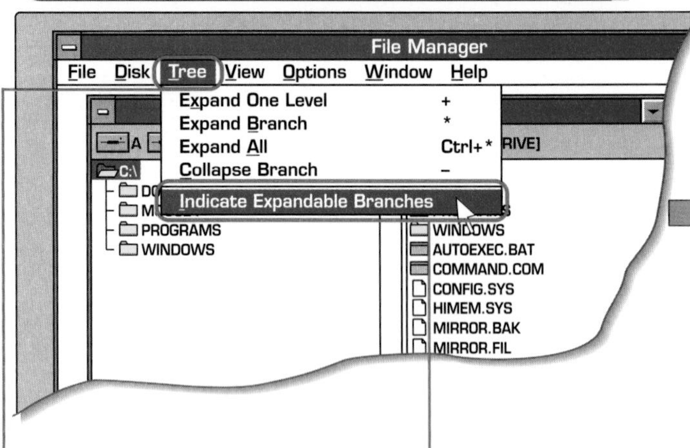

1 To turn on the **Indicate Expandable Branches** command, move the mouse over **Tree** and then press the left button.

*Note: A check mark (✓) in front of **Indicate Expandable Branches** indicates the command is **on**. To leave the command on, press* Alt.

2 To turn the command **on**, move the mouse over **Indicate Expandable Branches** and then press the left button.

Tip:

The **File Manager** takes longer to display a large directory tree when the **Indicate Expandable Branches** command is **on** (as opposed to **off**).

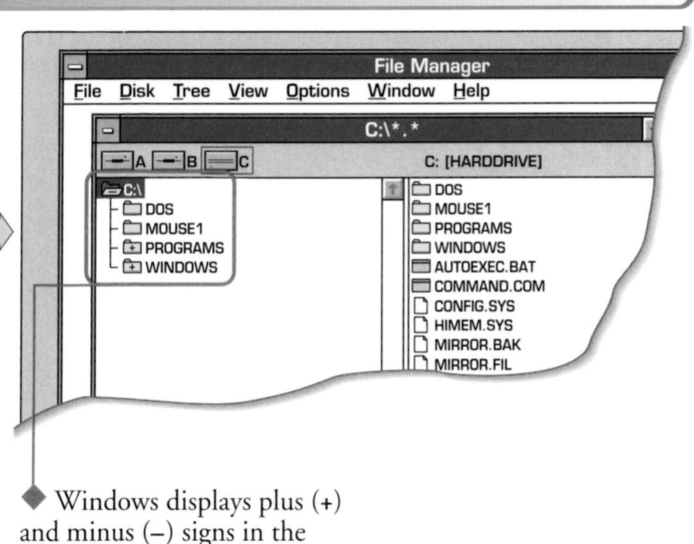

◆ Windows displays plus (+) and minus (–) signs in the directory folders that contain subdirectories.

CREATE A DIRECTORY

Create a Directory

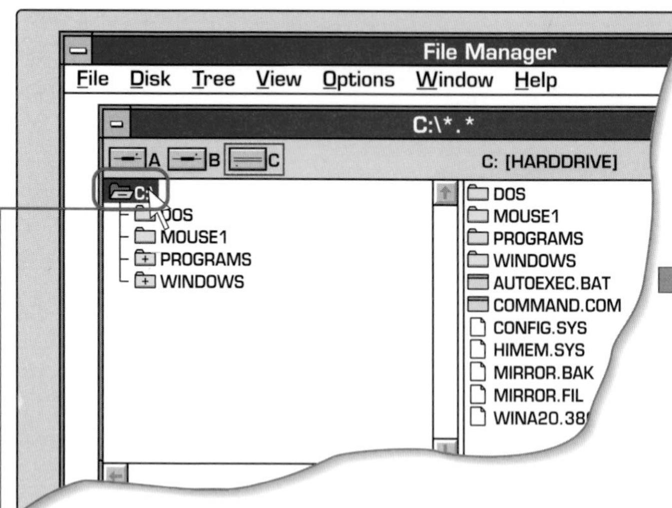

1 To select the directory you want to contain the new directory, move the mouse ↖ over its name (example: **C:**) and then press the left button.

Note: To open the ***File Manager****, refer to page 76.*

You can create directories to help you organize the programs and data stored on your hard and floppy drives.

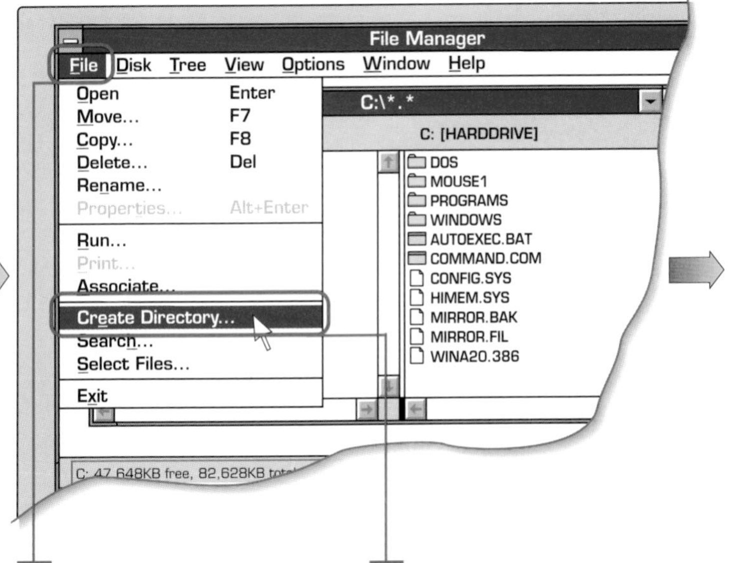

2 Move the mouse ↖ over **File** and then press the left button.

3 Move the mouse ↖ over **Create Directory** and then press the left button.

Note: To continue, refer to the next page.

Create a Directory (Continued)

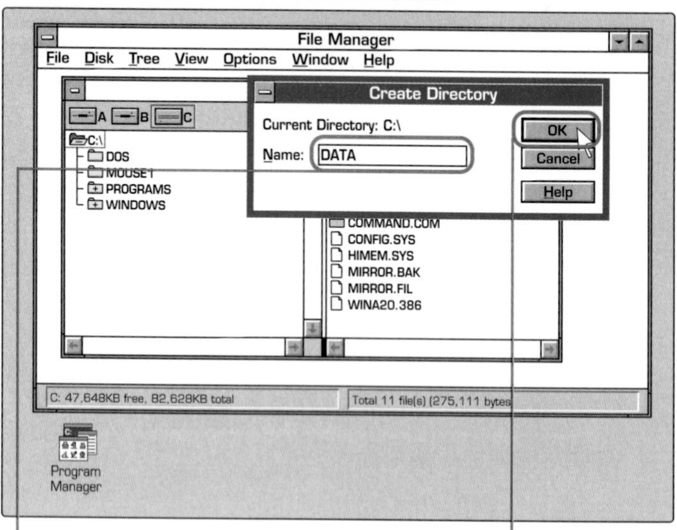

4 Type a name for the new directory (example: **DATA**).

5 Move the mouse over **OK** and then press the left button.

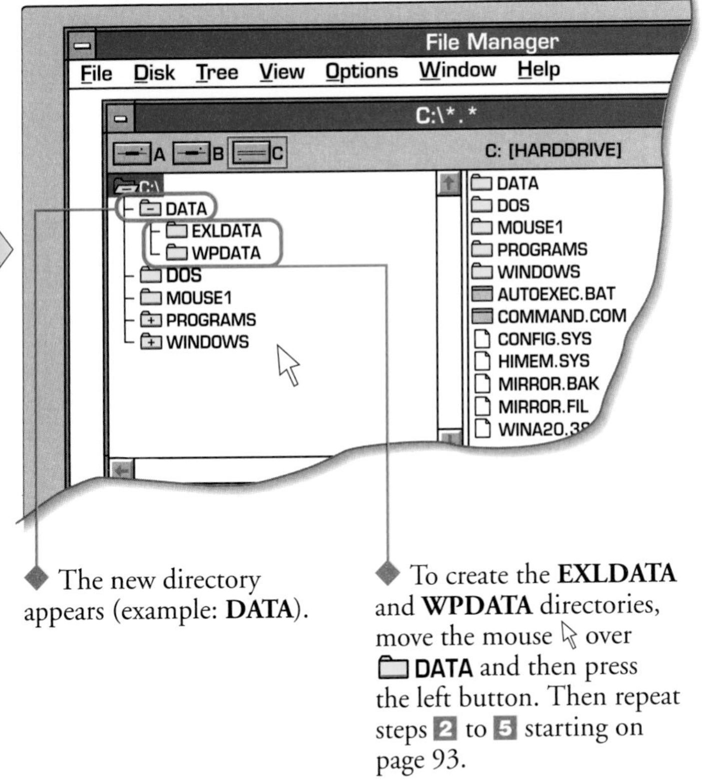

◆ The new directory appears (example: **DATA**).

◆ To create the **EXLDATA** and **WPDATA** directories, move the mouse over **DATA** and then press the left button. Then repeat steps **2** to **5** starting on page 93.

HIDE SUBDIRECTORIES

Hide Subdirectories

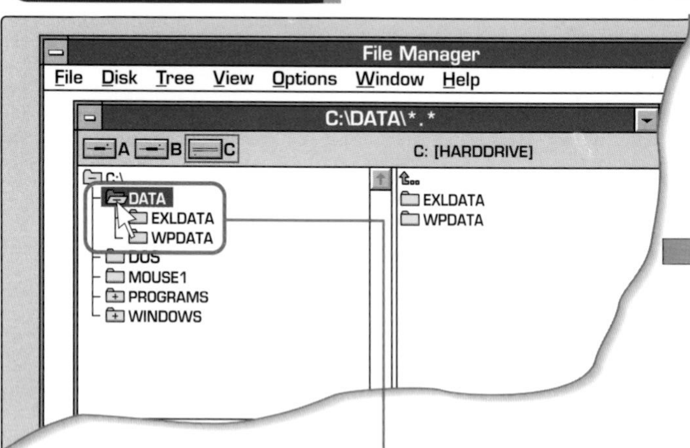

A minus sign (–) in a directory folder indicates that all of its subdirectories are displayed.

Note: To display plus (+) and minus (–) signs in directory folders, refer to page 90.

1 Move the mouse over the directory that contains the subdirectories you want to hide (example: **DATA**) and then quickly press the left button twice.

*Note: To open the **File Manager**, refer to page 76.*

You can hide all the subdirectories within a directory. This enables you to view directories more clearly by reducing the amount of information on your screen.

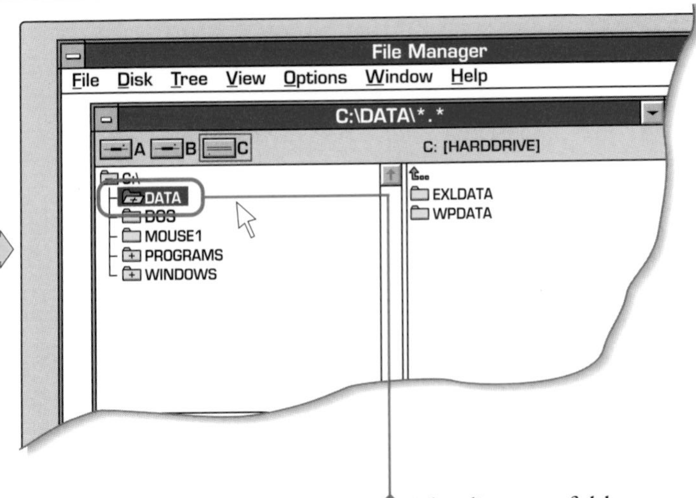

◆ All subdirectories in the current directory disappear from your screen.

◆ The directory folder now displays a plus sign (+). This indicates that all of its subdirectories are hidden.

DISPLAY SUBDIRECTORIES

Display Subdirectories (Expand One Level)

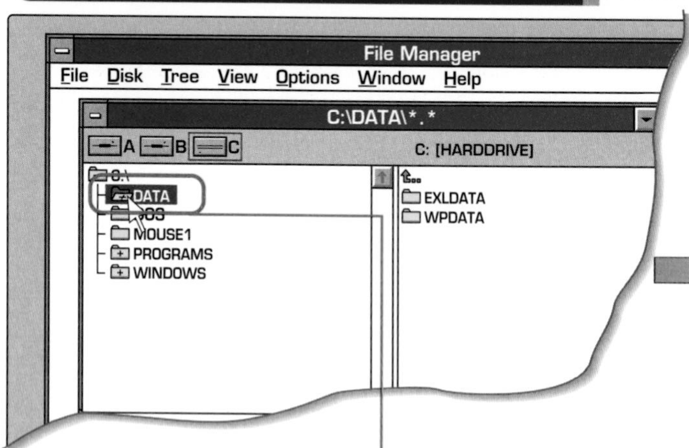

A plus sign (+) in a directory folder indicates that all of its subdirectories are hidden.

Note: To display plus (+) and minus (–) signs in directory folders, refer to page 90.

1 Move the mouse over the directory that contains the subdirectories you want to display (example: **DATA**) and then quickly press the left button twice.

*Note: To open the **File Manager**, refer to page 76.*

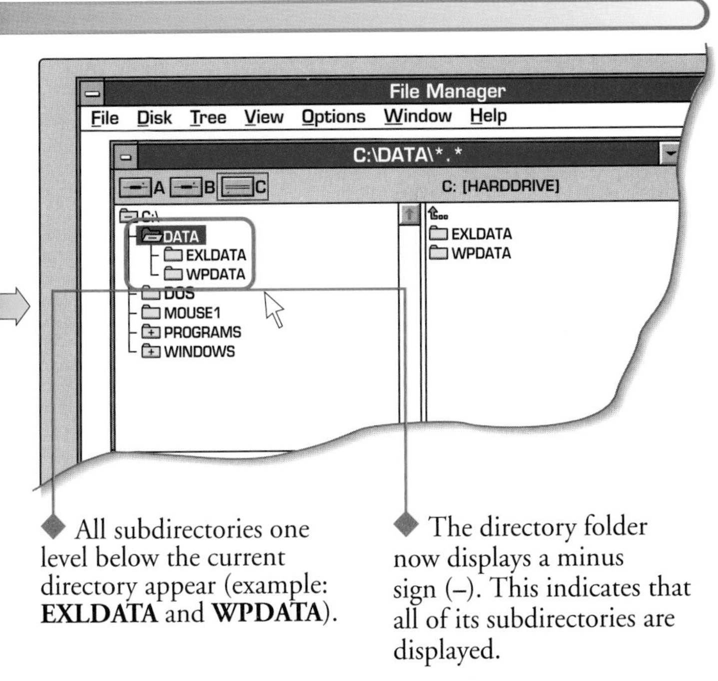

◆ All subdirectories one level below the current directory appear (example: **EXLDATA** and **WPDATA**).

◆ The directory folder now displays a minus sign (–). This indicates that all of its subdirectories are displayed.

DISPLAY SUBDIRECTORIES

Display Subdirectories (Expand Branch)

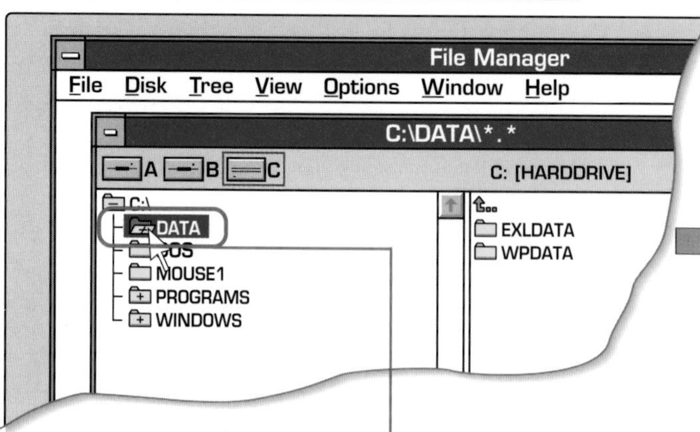

A plus sign (+) in a directory folder indicates that all of its subdirectories are hidden.

Note: To display plus (+) and minus (–) signs in directory folders, refer to page 90.

1 Move the mouse over the directory that contains the subdirectories you want to display (example: **DATA**) and then press the left button.

*Note: To open the **File Manager**, refer to page 76.*

You can display all the subdirectories in a directory.

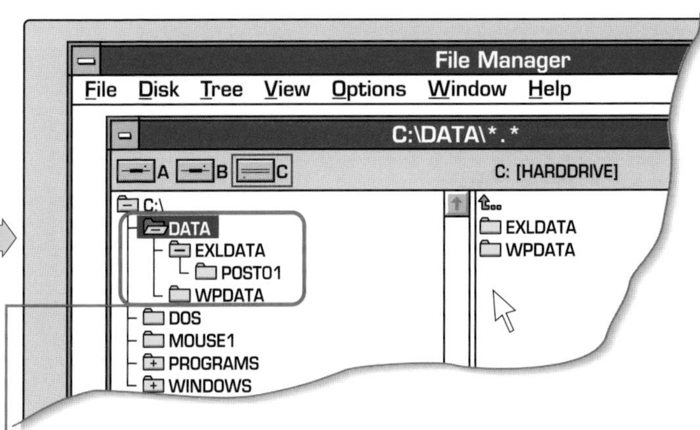

2 Press * and all subdirectories in the current directory appear.

◆ The directory folder now displays a minus sign (–). This indicates that all of its subdirectories are displayed.

Note: The subdirectory ***POST01*** *was created the same way as the* ***EXLDATA*** *and* ***WPDATA*** *subdirectories. To create a directory, refer to page 92.*

DISPLAY SUBDIRECTORIES

Display Subdirectories (Expand All)

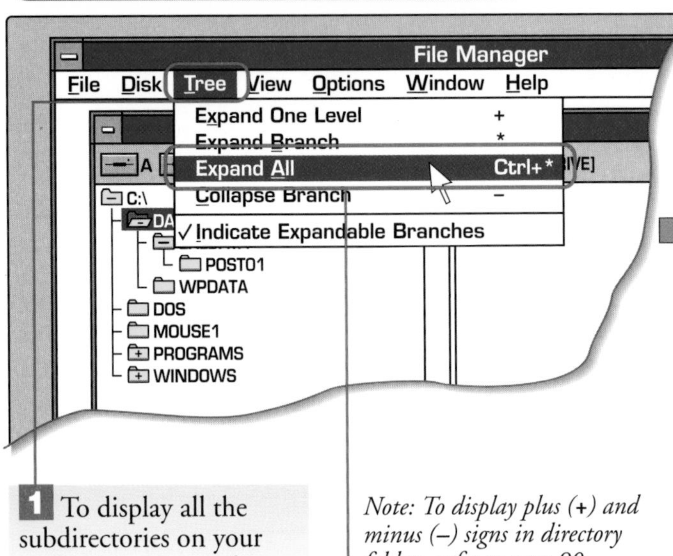

1 To display all the subdirectories on your entire drive, move the mouse over **Tree** and then press the left button.

Note: To display plus (+) and minus (–) signs in directory folders, refer to page 90.

2 Move the mouse over **Expand All** and then press the left button.

You can display all the subdirectories on your entire drive.

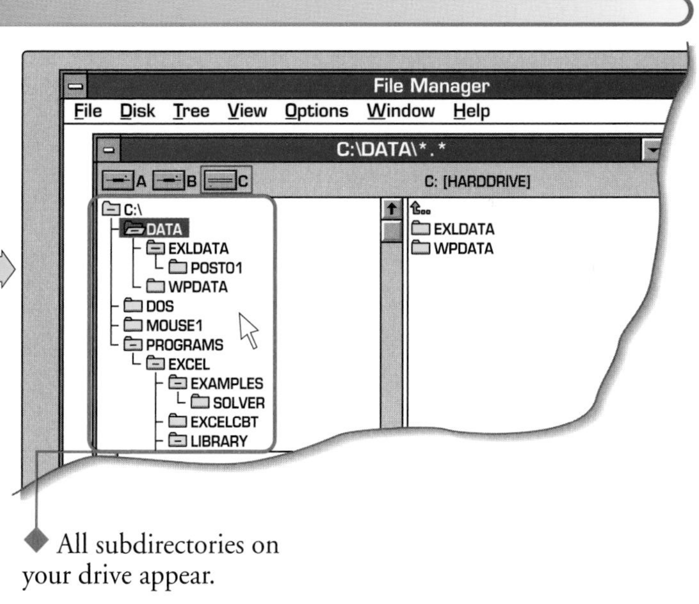

◆ All subdirectories on your drive appear.

MOVE A DIRECTORY

Move a Directory (Within the Same Drive)

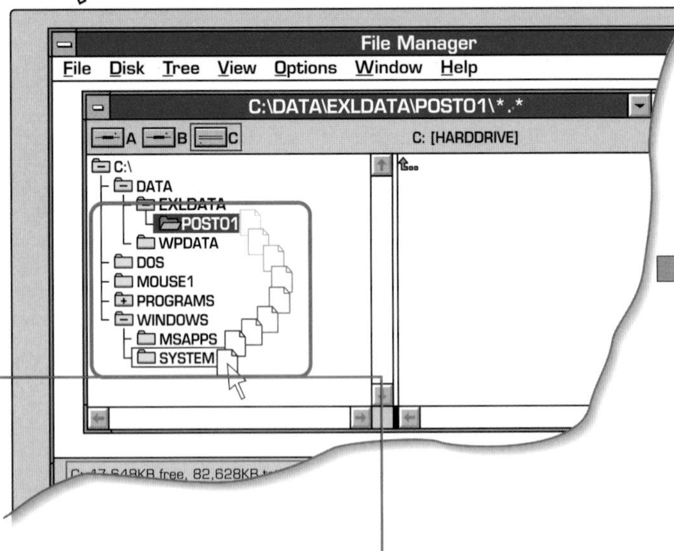

1 Move the mouse over the directory you want to move (example: **POST01**).

*Note: To open the **File Manager**, refer to page 76.*

2 Press and hold down the left button as you drag the directory to a new location. A rectangle appears around the destination directory (example: SYSTEM).

You can move a directory to a new location. The directory disappears from its original place.

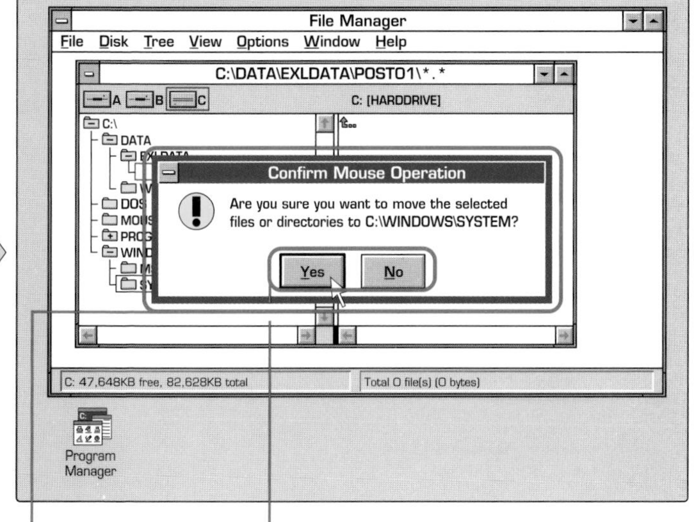

3 Release the left button and this dialog box appears.

4 To move the directory, position the mouse over **Yes** and then press the left button.

◆ To cancel the move, position the mouse over **No** and then press the left button.

Note: To continue, refer to the next page.

MOVE A DIRECTORY

Move a Directory (Continued)

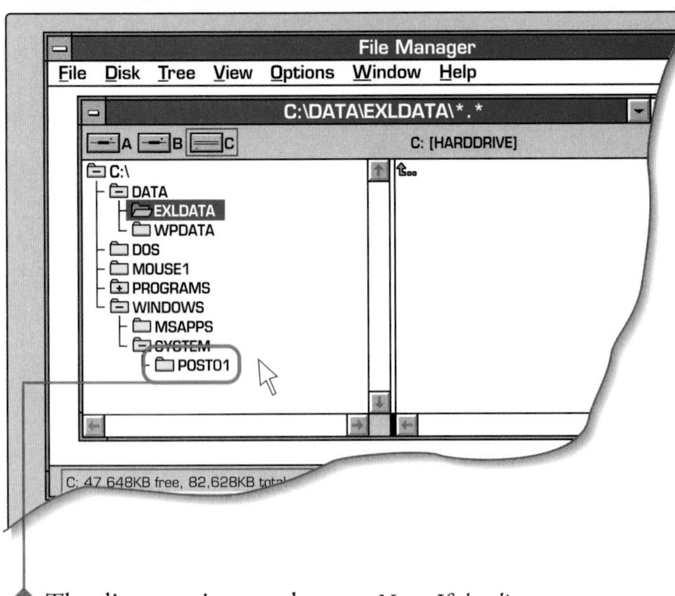

◆ The directory is moved.

Note: If the directory you moved contains files, these are also moved.

CAUTION:

Only move directories that you have created for storing data files. Moving a directory containing program files may cause problems (example: do not move the **WINDOWS** directory).

MOVE A DIRECTORY (TO A DIFFERENT DRIVE)

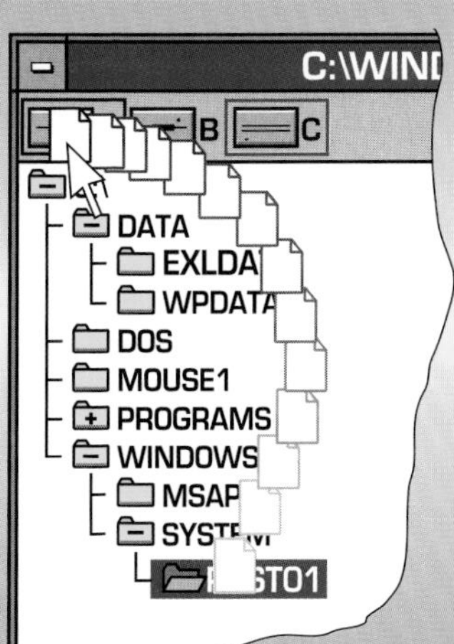

Repeat steps 1 to 4 starting on page 104, except press and hold down Alt before performing step 2.

Note: If you want to move a directory to a floppy drive, make sure you first insert a diskette into the drive.

COPY A DIRECTORY

Copy a Directory *(Within the Same Drive)*

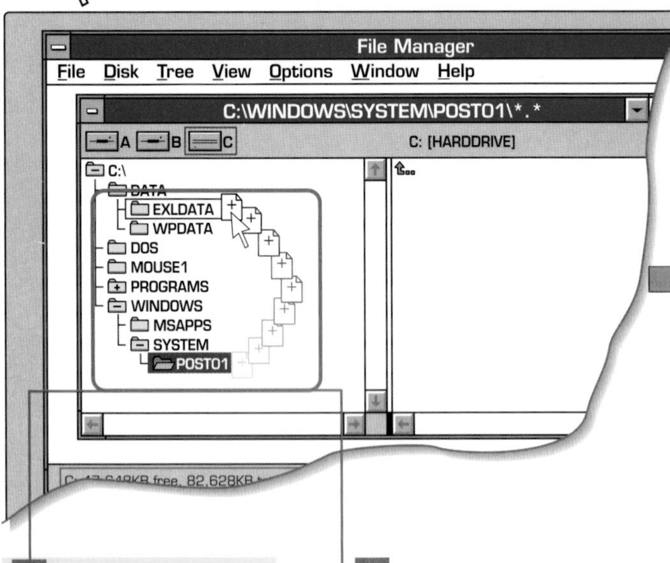

1 Move the mouse over the directory you want to copy (example: **POST01**).

Note: To open the ***File Manager****, refer to page 76.*

2 Press and hold down Ctrl.

3 Still holding down Ctrl, press and hold down the left button as you drag the directory to a new location. A rectangle appears around the destination directory (example: EXLDATA).

You can copy a directory and then paste the copy in a new location. The original directory remains in its place.

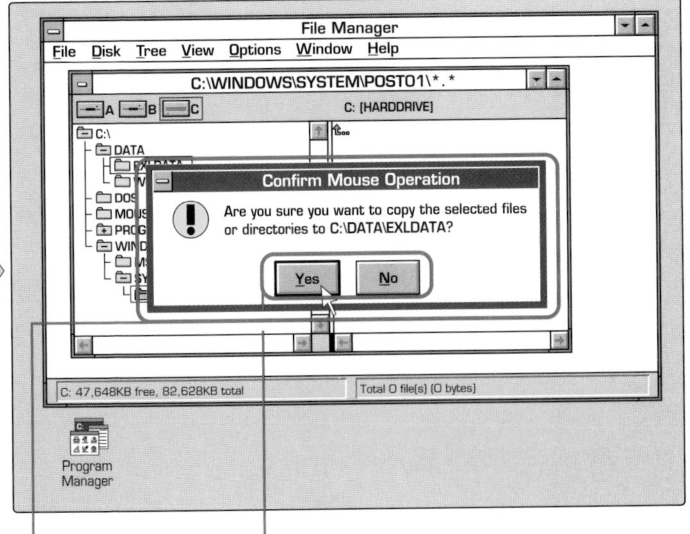

4 Release the left button and then release Ctrl. This dialog box appears.

5 To copy the directory, move the mouse over **Yes** and then press the left button.

◆ To cancel the copy, move the mouse over **No** and then press the left button.

Note: To continue, refer to the next page.

COPY A DIRECTORY

Copy a Directory (Continued)

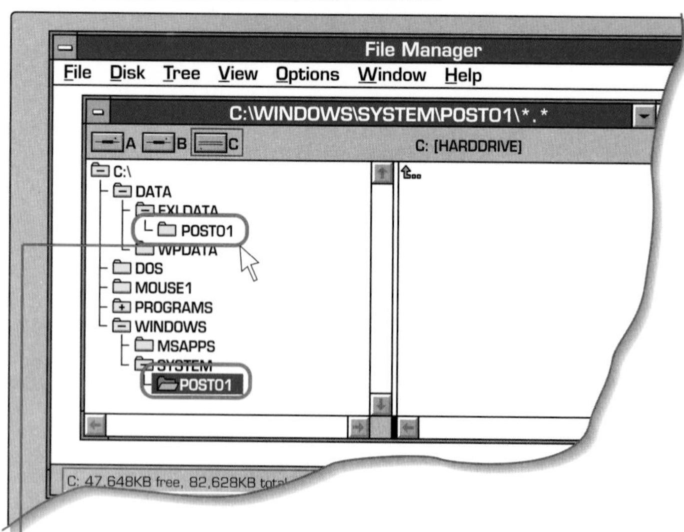

- The directory is copied.

Note: If the directory you copied contains files, these are also copied.

You can copy a directory to another directory or drive.

COPY A DIRECTORY (TO A DIFFERENT DRIVE)

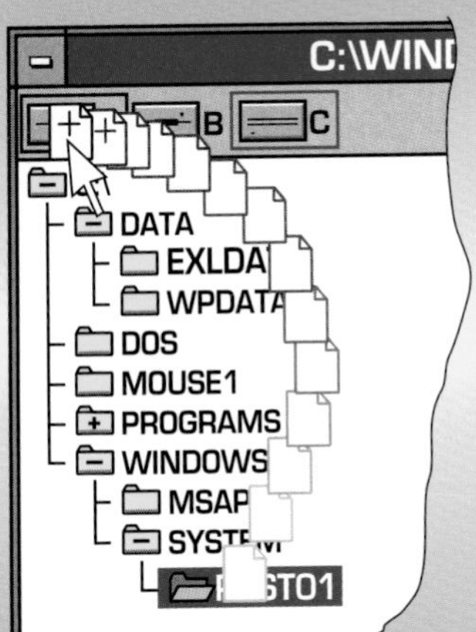

Repeat steps 1 to 5 starting on page 108, except do not press and hold down Ctrl in steps 2 and 3.

Note: If you want to copy a directory to a floppy drive, make sure you first insert a diskette into the drive.

DELETE A DIRECTORY

Delete a Directory

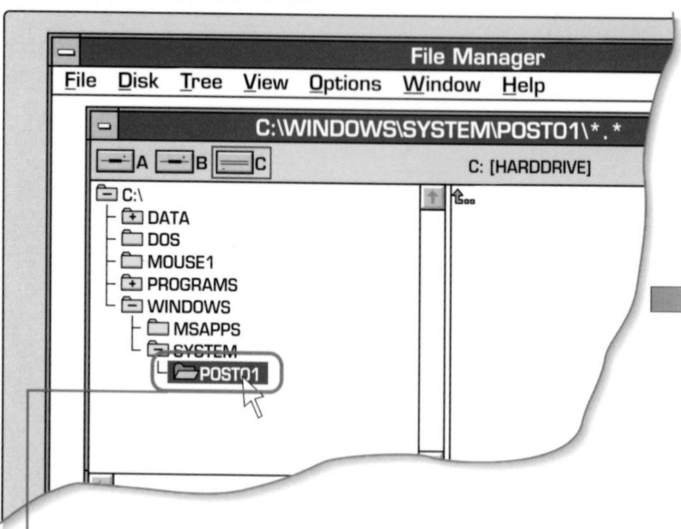

1 Move the mouse over the directory you want to delete (example: **POST01**) and then press the left button.

Note: To open the ***File Manager****, refer to page 76.*

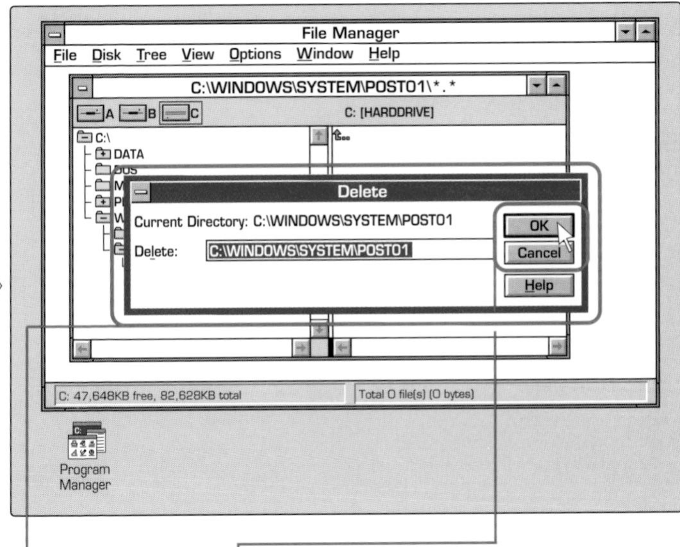

2 Press Delete and the **Delete** dialog box appears.

3 To delete the directory, move the mouse over **OK** and then press the left button.

◆ To cancel the deletion, move the mouse over **Cancel** and then press the left button.

Note: To continue, refer to the next page.

DELETE A DIRECTORY

Delete a Directory (Continued)

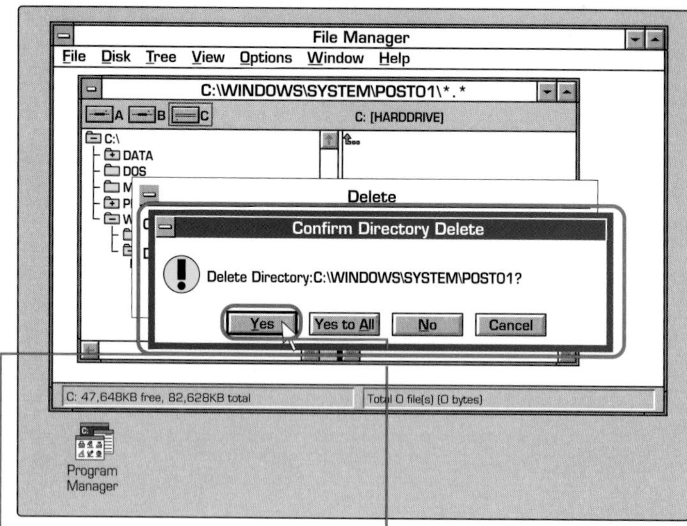

◆ Once you delete a directory, it is **permanently erased** from your drive. This dialog box offers you a final chance to cancel the deletion.

4 To delete the directory, move the mouse over **Yes** and then press the left button.

Note: If the directory you are deleting contains files, refer to the top of page 115.

This dialog box appears if the directory you are deleting contains files.

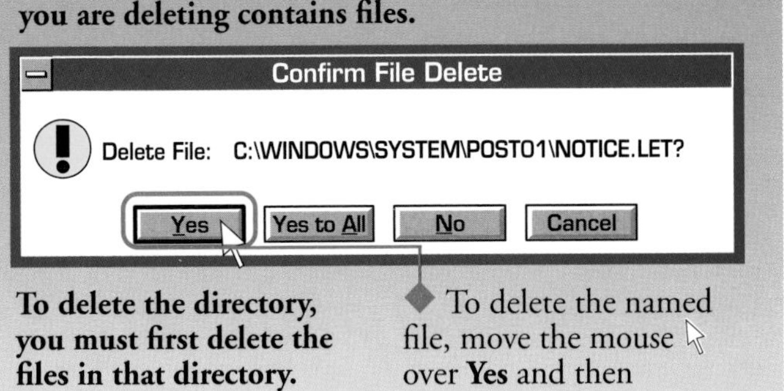

To delete the directory, you must first delete the files in that directory.

◆ To delete the named file, move the mouse over **Yes** and then press the left button.

◆ The directory is deleted from your drive.

◆ The File Manager displays a symbol beside each file to indicate the file type.

◆ This symbol represents a document file. These files are associated with applications.

◆ This symbol represents a system or hidden file.

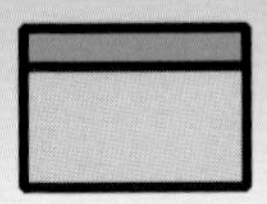

◆ This symbol represents a program file, PIF or batch file. These files start applications.

◆ This symbol represents all other files.

FILE NAMES

File Names

A file name consists of two parts: a name and an extension. You must separate these parts with a period.

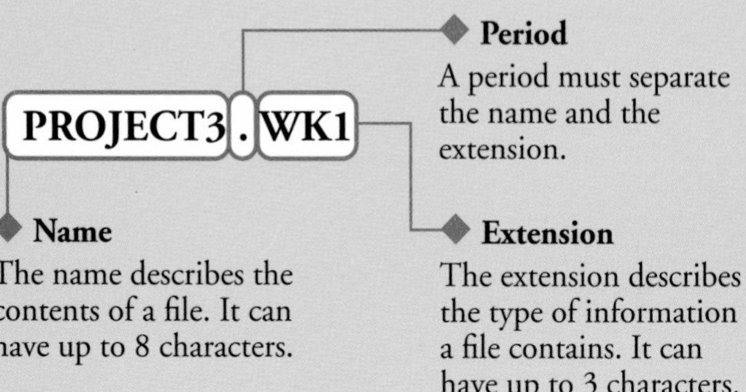

Period
A period must separate the name and the extension.

Name
The name describes the contents of a file. It can have up to 8 characters.

Extension
The extension describes the type of information a file contains. It can have up to 3 characters.

COMMON EXTENSIONS

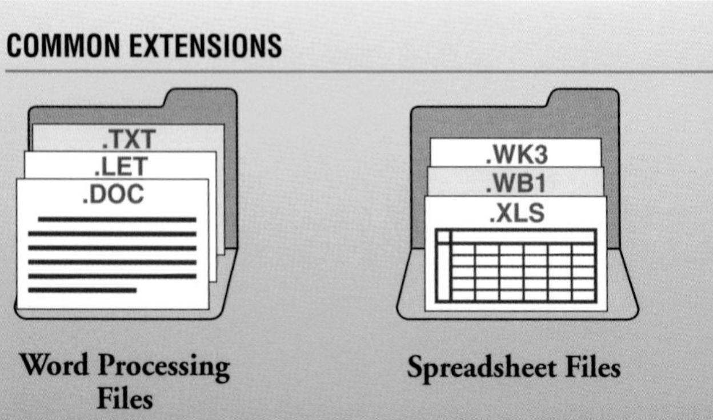

Word Processing Files

Spreadsheet Files

RULES FOR NAMING A FILE

A file name can contain the following characters:

- The letters A to Z, upper or lower case
- The numbers 0 through 9
- The symbols _ ^ $ ~ ! # % & - { } @ ( )

Note: A file name cannot contain a period, blank space or comma.

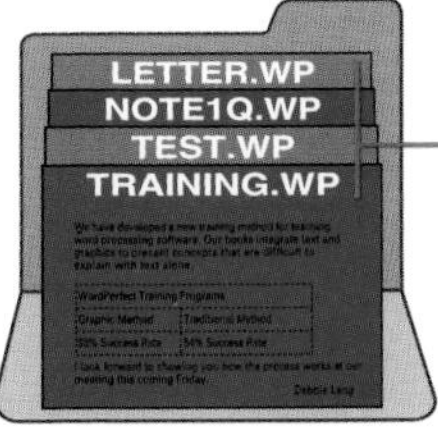

- Each file in a directory must have a unique name.

Program Files

SPLIT A DIRECTORY WINDOW

If there is not enough space to view all your files or directories, you can adjust the size of the display areas.

Split a Directory Window

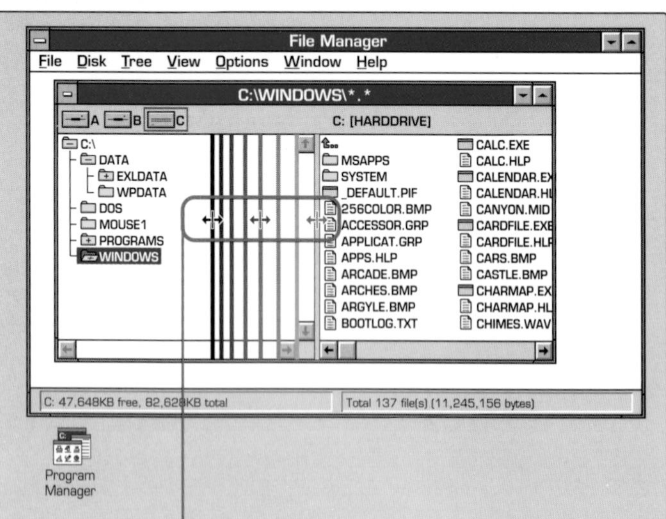

1 Move the mouse ↖ over the line to the left of the file names and ↖ changes to ↔.

*Note: To open the **File Manager**, refer to page 76.*

2 Press and hold down the left button as you move the vertical line to a new position.

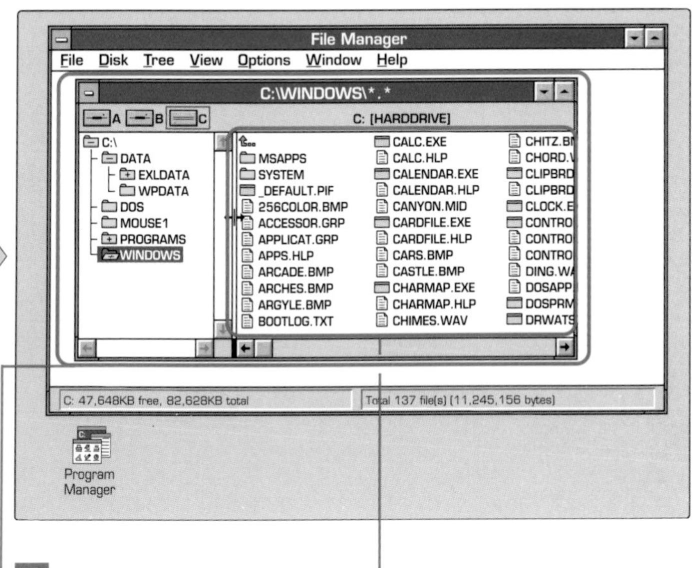

3 Release the left button and the window splits at the position you specified.

◆ In this example, there is now more space to display the names of the files in the current directory.

TREE AND DIRECTORY VIEWS

Tree and Directory

◆ This is the initial (or default) setting. Both the directory tree and the contents of the current directory are displayed.

*Note: To open the **File Manager**, refer to page 76.*

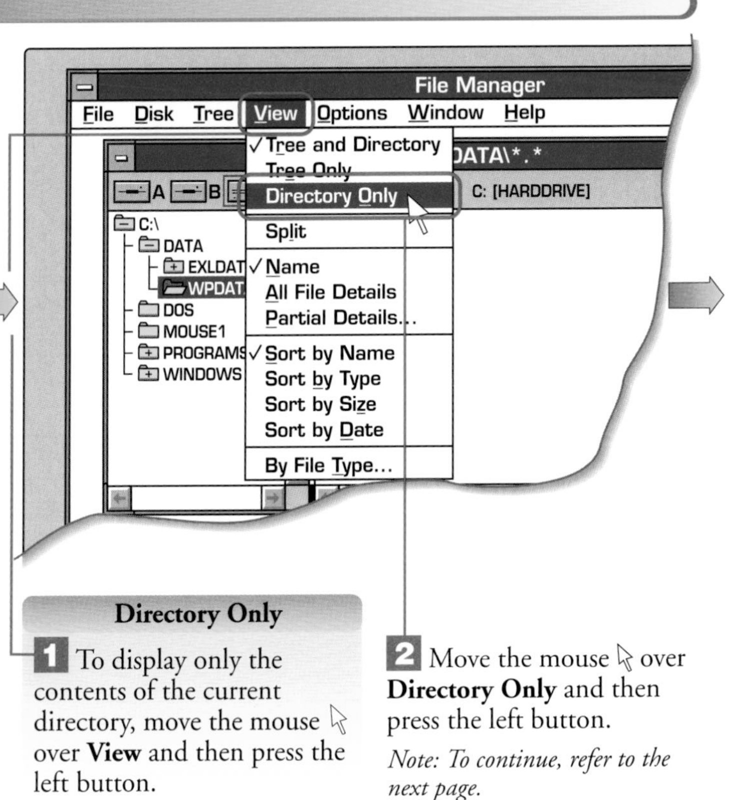

Directory Only

1 To display only the contents of the current directory, move the mouse over **View** and then press the left button.

2 Move the mouse over **Directory Only** and then press the left button.

Note: To continue, refer to the next page.

TREE AND DIRECTORY VIEWS

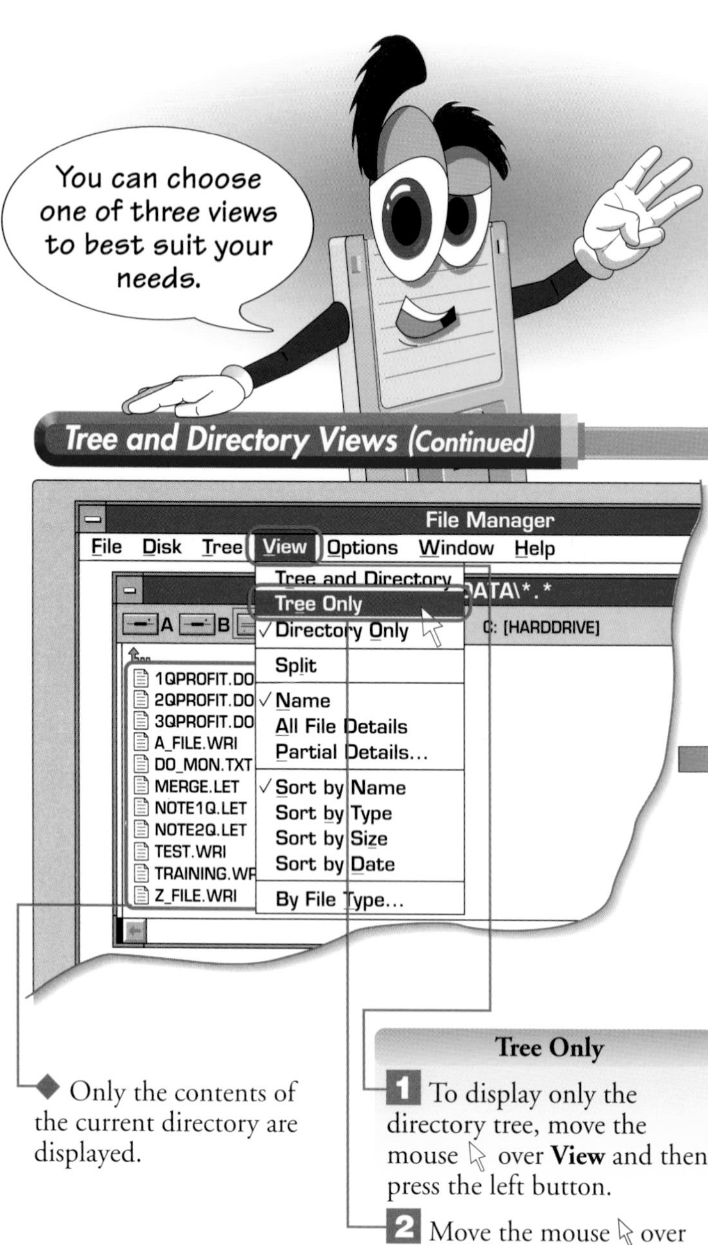

◆ Only the contents of the current directory are displayed.

Tree Only

1 To display only the directory tree, move the mouse ↖ over **View** and then press the left button.

2 Move the mouse ↖ over **Tree Only** and then press the left button.

TREE AND DIRECTORY

1 To display both the directory tree and the contents of the current directory, move the mouse over **View** and then press the left button.

2 Move the mouse over **Tree and Directory** and then press the left button.

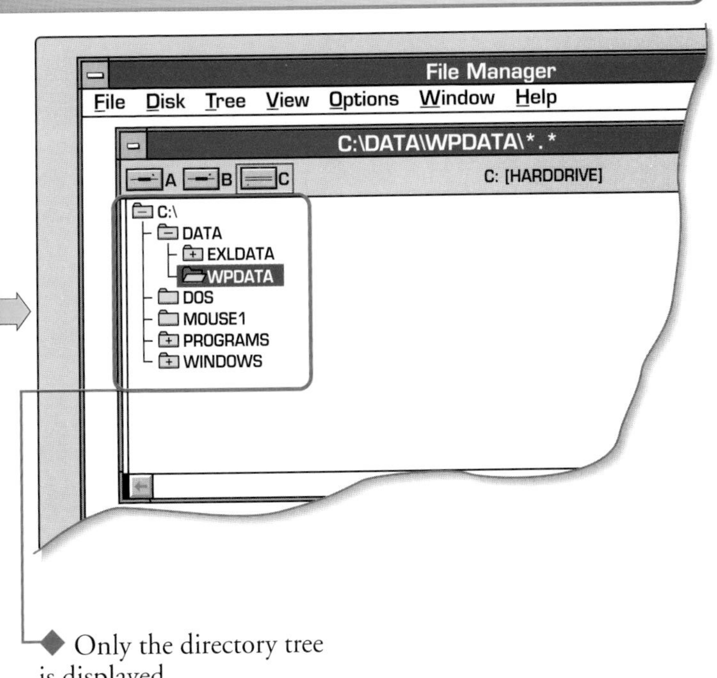

◆ Only the directory tree is displayed.

DISPLAY FILE INFORMATION

You can obtain information about the files on your screen. Windows can display the following details:

Display File Information

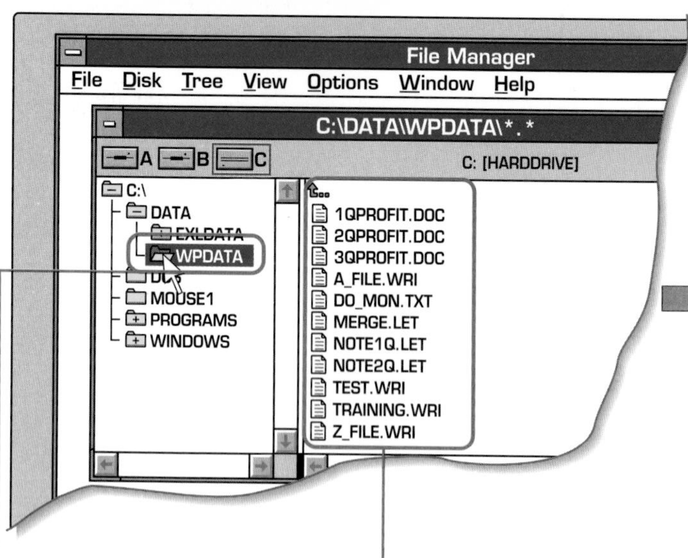

1 Move the mouse over the directory that contains the files you want to display (example: **WPDATA**) and then press the left button.

*Note: To open the **File Manager**, refer to page 76.*

◆ The files in the selected directory appear.

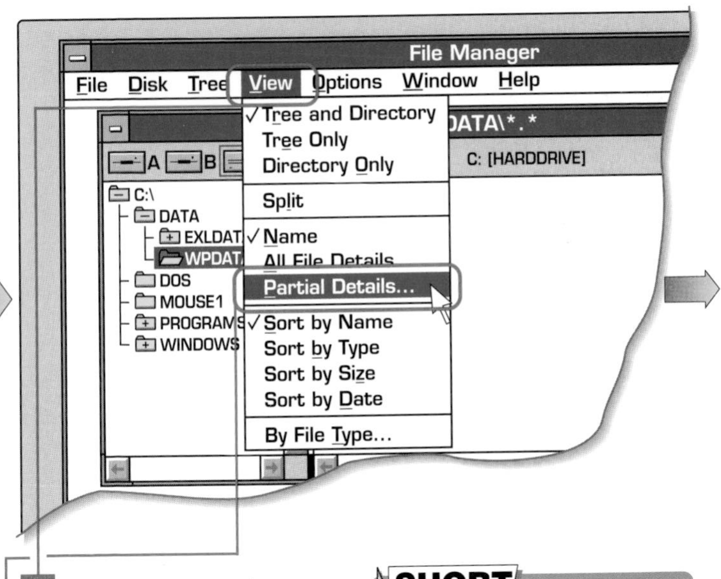

2 Move the mouse over **View** and then press the left button.

3 Move the mouse over **Partial Details** and then press the left button.

Note: To continue, refer to the next page.

DISPLAY FILE INFORMATION

Display File Information (Continued)

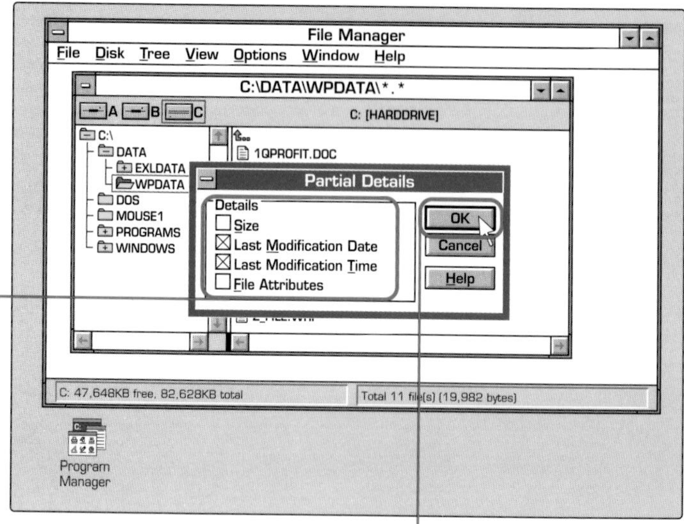

◆ The **Partial Details** dialog box appears.

4 Move the mouse ⇖ over the box beside a file detail you want to display and then press the left button (☐ becomes ☒).

5 Repeat step **4** for each file detail you want to display.

6 Move the mouse ⇖ over **OK** and then press the left button.

DISPLAY ONLY FILE NAMES

To simplify your screen, you can display the name of each file and hide all other file details.

1 Move the mouse over **View** and then press the left button.

2 Move the mouse over **Name** and then press the left button.

Note: This is the initial (or default) setting.

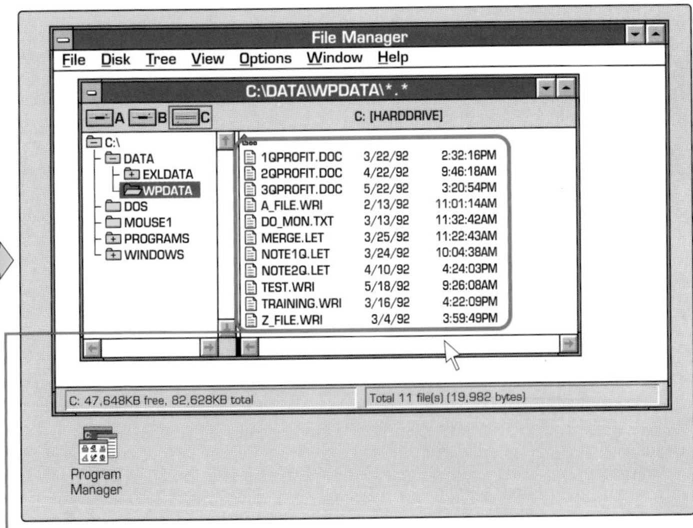

◆ Each file now displays the details you selected.

SORT FILES

C:\DATA\WPDATA*.*
A
B
C
C: [HARDDRIVE]
C:\
DATA
EXLDATA
WPDATA
DOS
MOUSE1
PROGRAMS
WHAP
DATE
1
2

You can sort files by name, type, size or date.
MERGE
Name of the file
Size of the file
.LET
File type or extension
March 19
Date the file was created or last modified

You can change the order of the files displayed on your screen by using the Sort command.

Sort Files

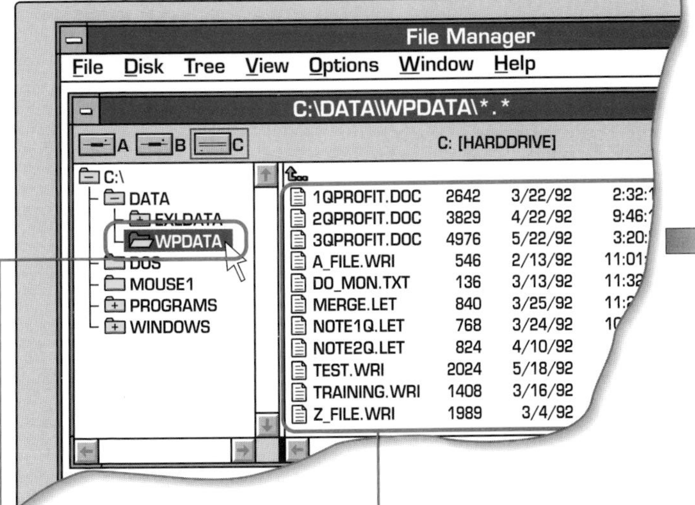

1 Move the mouse over the directory that contains the files you want to sort (example: **WPDATA**) and then press the left button.

Note: To open the ***File Manager****, refer to page 76.*

◆ The files in the selected directory appear.

Note: To continue, refer to the next page.

SORT FILES

Sort Files (Continued)

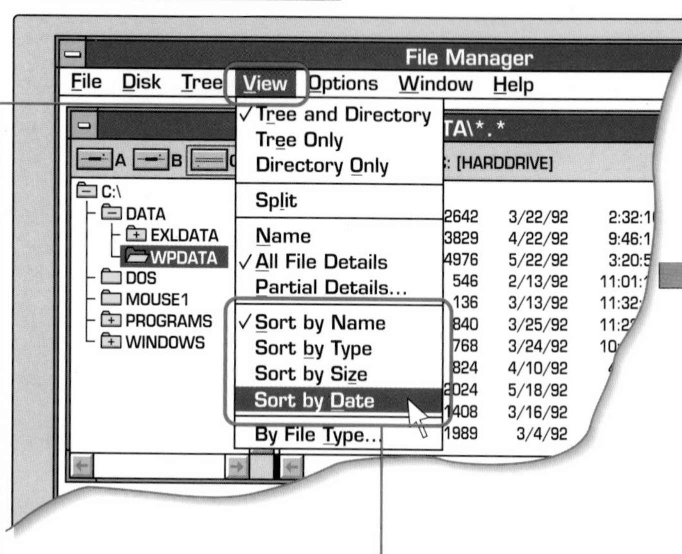

2 To sort the files, move the mouse over **View** and then press the left button.

3 Move the mouse over the sort command you want to use (example: **Sort by Date**) and then press the left button.

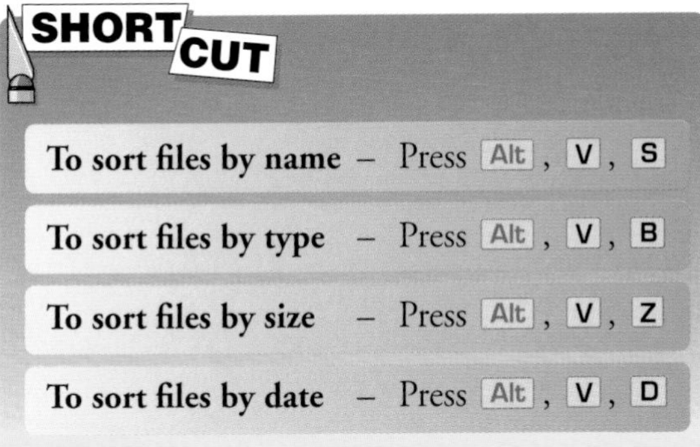

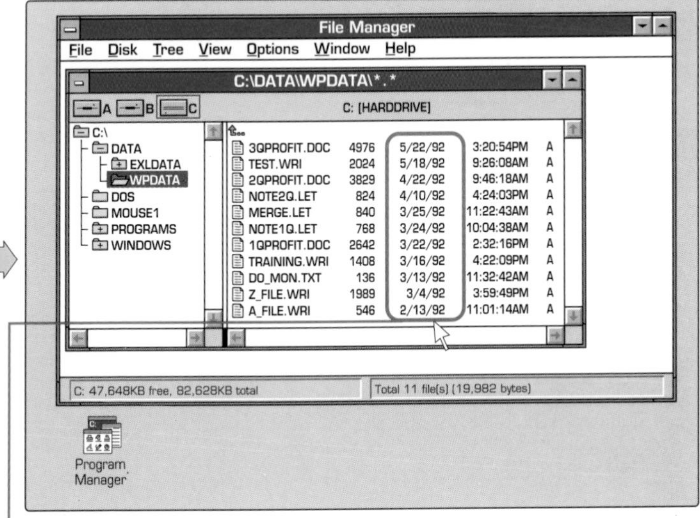

◆ In this example, the files are sorted by date. The most recently created or modified files appear first.

WILDCARDS

Using the ? Wildcard

The question mark (?) represents a single character in a file name.

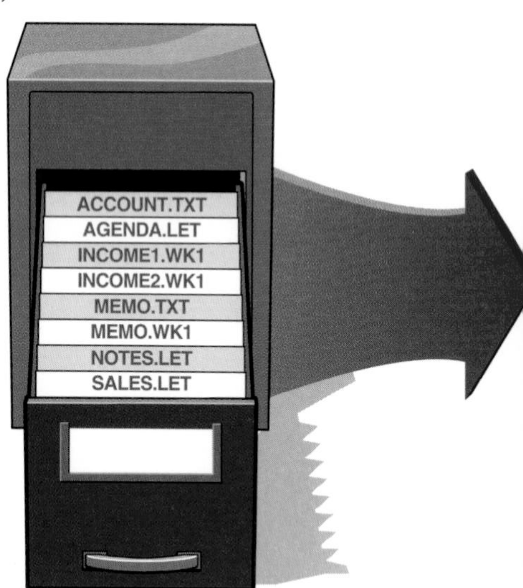

Wildcards let you work on files with related names at the same time. This enables you to select, copy, move, delete and search for files in less time.

Windows recognizes two wildcards: the question mark (?) and the asterisk (*).

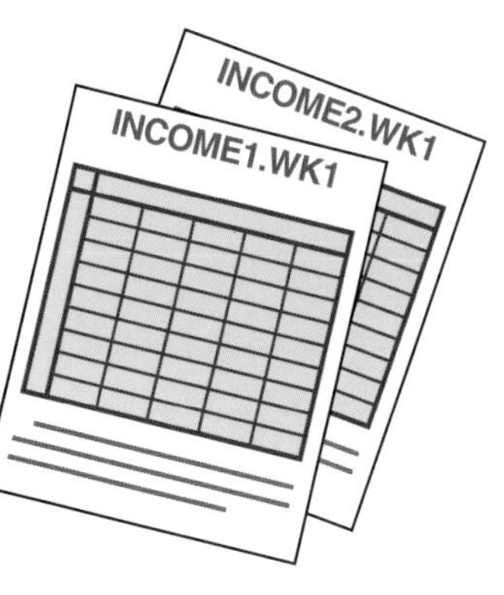

INCOME?.WK1 includes all files starting with **INCOME**, followed by any single character and then ending with the **.WK1** extension.

Note: A file named ***INCOME1A.WK1*** *would not be included.*

WILDCARDS

Using the * Wildcard

The asterisk (*) represents one or more characters in a file name.

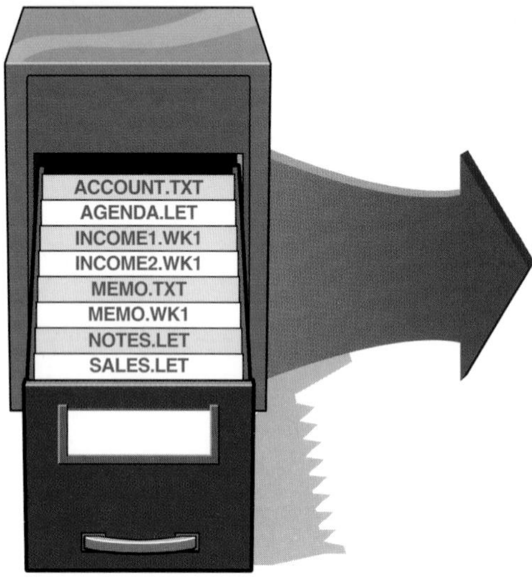

MEMO.* includes all files named **MEMO**, with any extension.

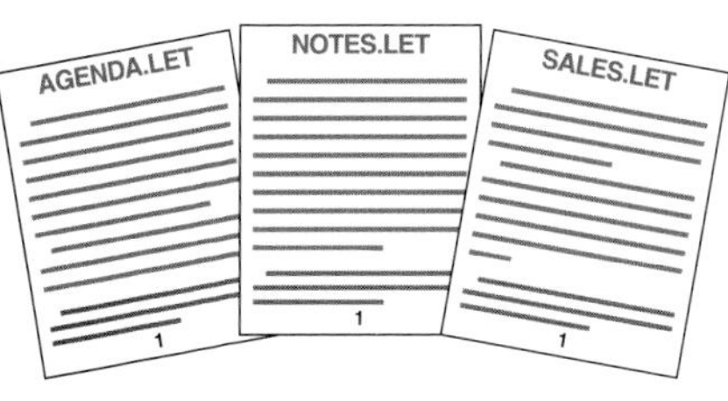

***.LET** includes all files with the **LET** extension.

OTHER EXAMPLES:

A*.* includes all files starting with the letter **A**, with any extension.

. includes all files.

SEARCH FOR FILES

Search for Files

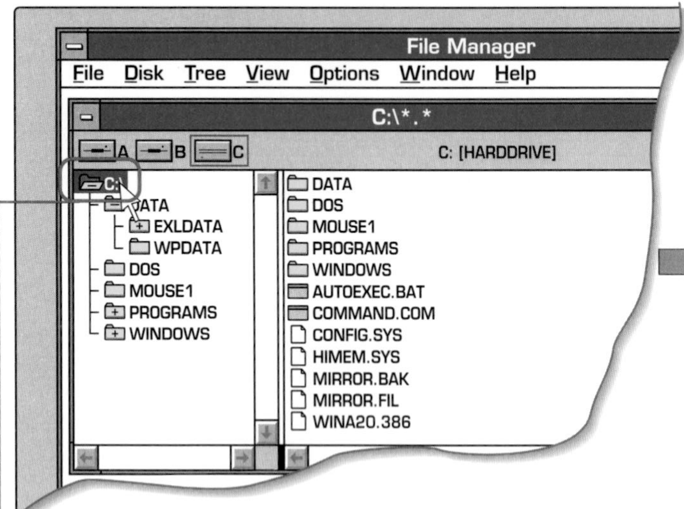

1 Move the mouse over the directory you want to search (example: **C:**) and then press the left button.

Note: To open the ***File Manager****, refer to page 76.*

◆ Windows will search the current directory and all of its subdirectories.

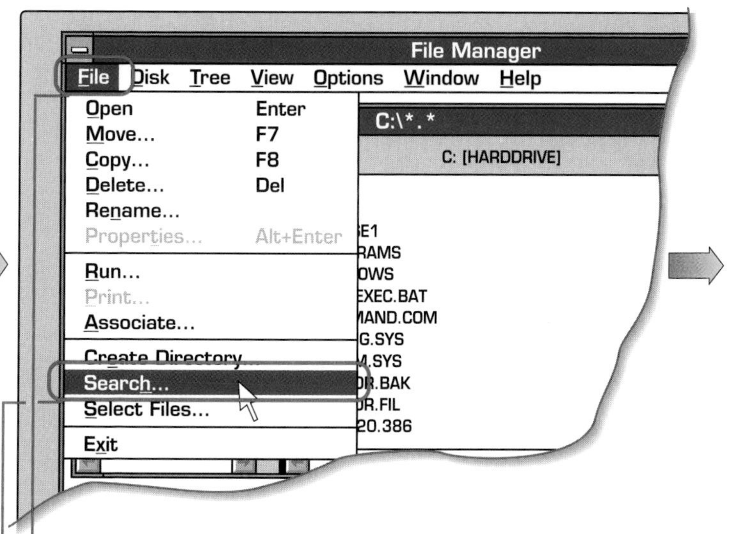

2 Move the mouse over **File** and then press the left button.

3 Move the mouse over **Search** and then press the left button.

Note: To continue, refer to the next page.

Search for Files (Continued)

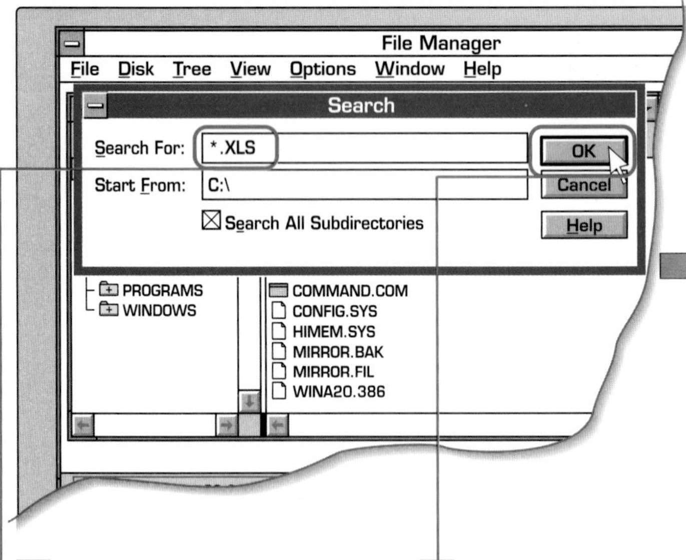

4 Specify the files you want to search for by using the wildcard characters (example: type ***.XLS** to search for all files with the **XLS** extension).

*Note: If you know the name of the file you want to search for, type the file name (example: type **INCOME1Q.XLS**).*

5 To start the search, move the mouse over **OK** and then press the left button.

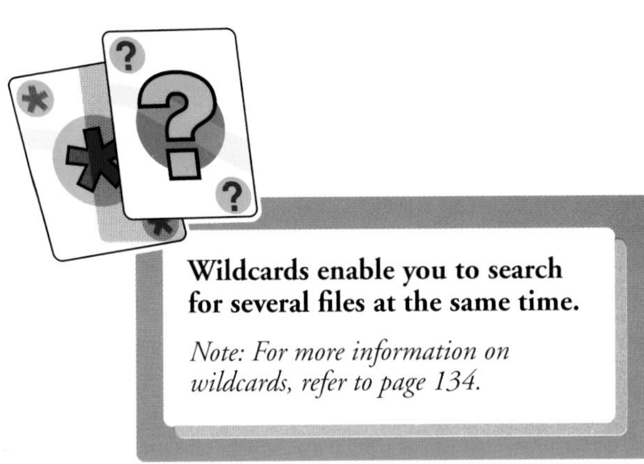

Wildcards enable you to search for several files at the same time.

Note: For more information on wildcards, refer to page 134.

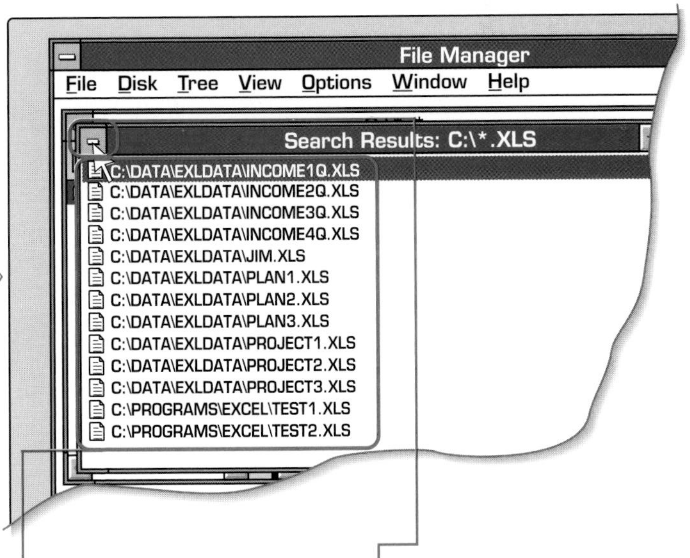

File Manager
File Disk Tree View Options Window Help
Search Results: C:*.XLS
C:\DATA\EXLDATA\INCOME1Q.XLS
C:\DATA\EXLDATA\INCOME2Q.XLS
C:\DATA\EXLDATA\INCOME3Q.XLS
C:\DATA\EXLDATA\INCOME4Q.XLS
C:\DATA\EXLDATA\JIM.XLS
C:\DATA\EXLDATA\PLAN1.XLS
C:\DATA\EXLDATA\PLAN2.XLS
C:\DATA\EXLDATA\PLAN3.XLS
C:\DATA\EXLDATA\PROJECT1.XLS
C:\DATA\EXLDATA\PROJECT2.XLS
C:\DATA\EXLDATA\PROJECT3.XLS
C:\PROGRAMS\EXCEL\TEST1.XLS
C:\PROGRAMS\EXCEL\TEST2.XLS

◆ The **Search Results** window appears listing all files with matching file names.

6 To close the **Search Results** window, move the mouse over its **control-menu box** and then quickly press the left button twice.

SELECT FILES

Select Files Randomly

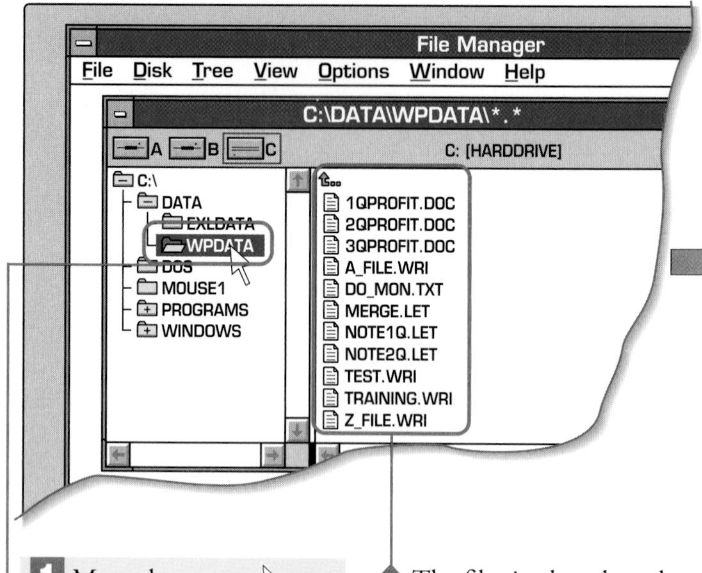

1 Move the mouse over the directory that contains the files you want to select (example: **WPDATA**) and then press the left button.

*Note: To open the **File Manager**, refer to page 76.*

◆ The files in the selected directory appear.

To copy, move or delete files, you must first select the files you want to work with. Selected files appear highlighted on your screen.

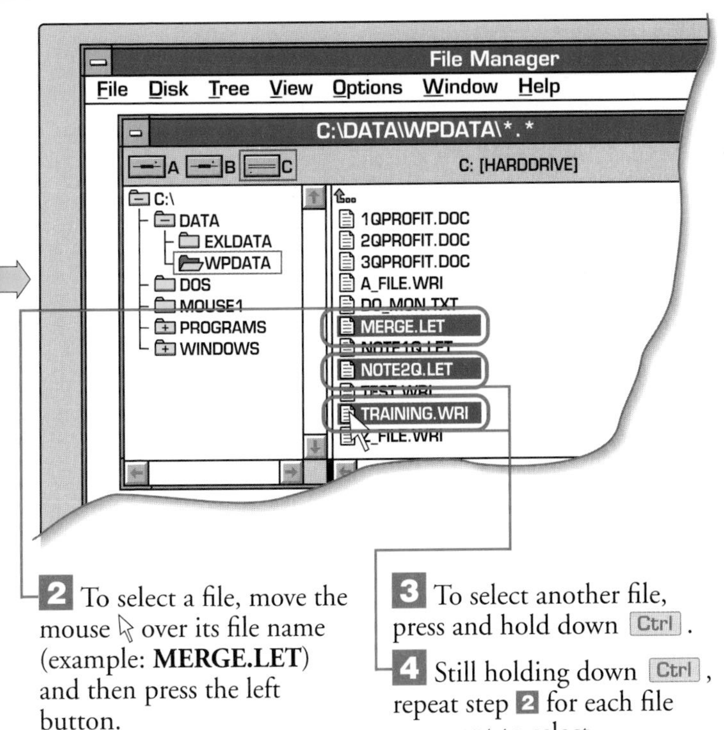

2 To select a file, move the mouse over its file name (example: **MERGE.LET**) and then press the left button.

3 To select another file, press and hold down Ctrl.

4 Still holding down Ctrl, repeat step **2** for each file you want to select.

SELECT FILES

Select a Group of Files in a Sequence

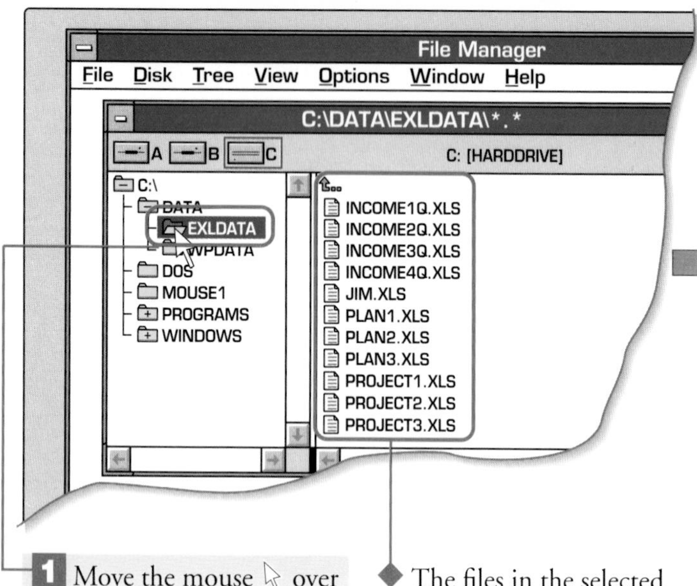

1 Move the mouse over the directory that contains the files you want to select (example: **EXLDATA**) and then press the left button.

Note: To open the ***File Manager****, refer to page 76.*

◆ The files in the selected directory appear.

Windows lets you easily select groups of files. This enables you to copy, move or delete several files at the same time. Selected files appear highlighted on your screen.

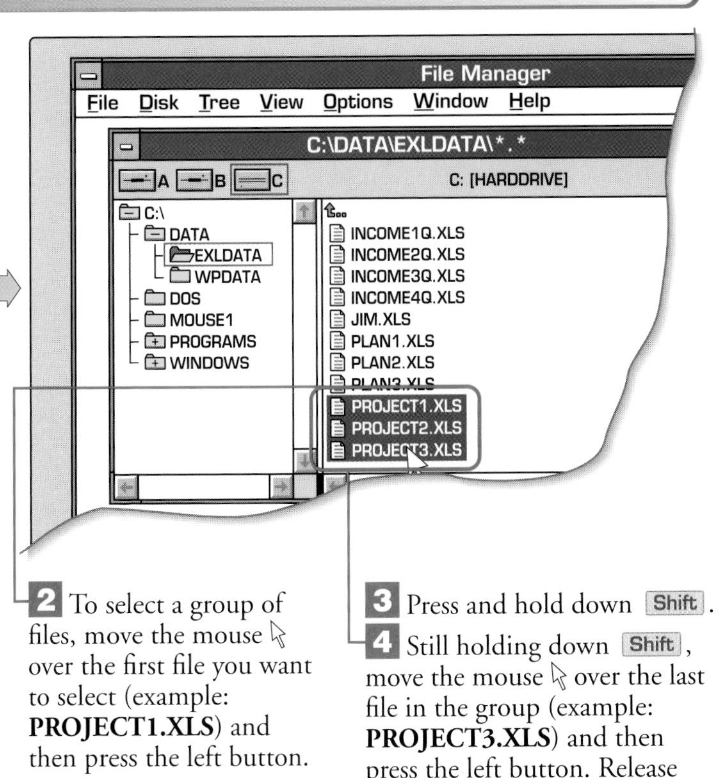

2 To select a group of files, move the mouse ⇖ over the first file you want to select (example: **PROJECT1.XLS**) and then press the left button.

3 Press and hold down Shift.

4 Still holding down Shift, move the mouse ⇖ over the last file in the group (example: **PROJECT3.XLS**) and then press the left button. Release Shift.

SELECT FILES

Select Files Using Wildcard Characters

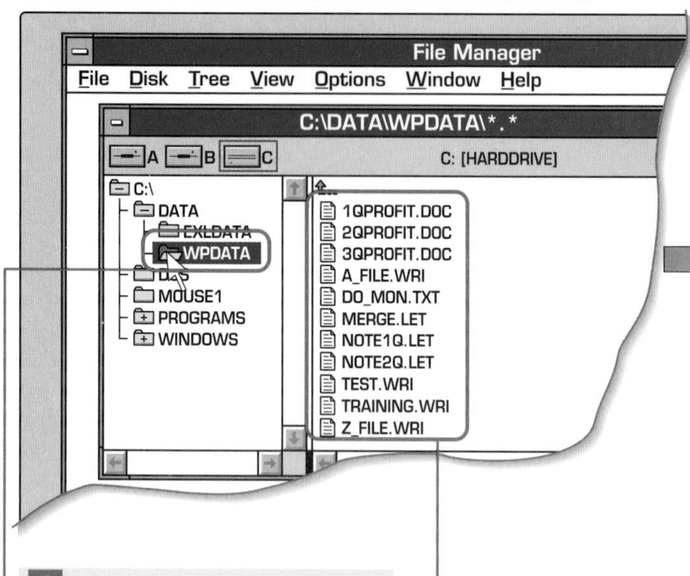

1 Move the mouse over the directory that contains the files you want to select (example: **WPDATA**) and then press the left button.

Note: To open the ***File Manager****, refer to page 76.*

◆ The files in the selected directory appear.

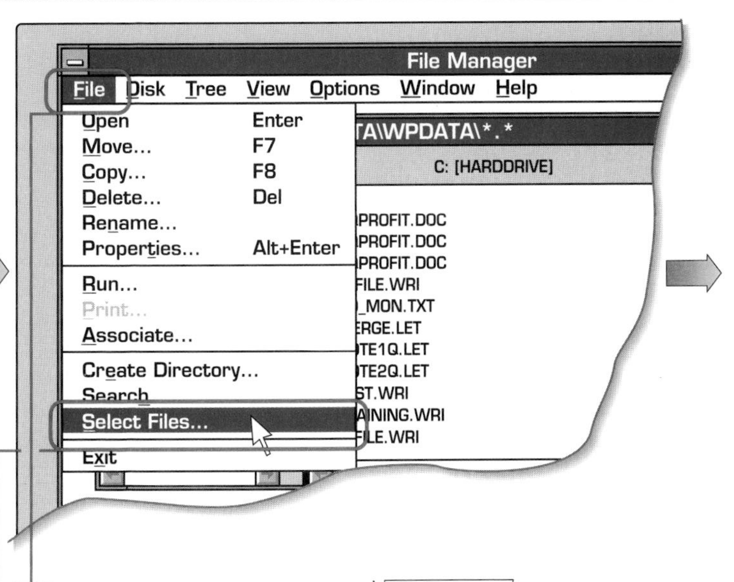

2 Move the mouse over **File** and then press the left button.

3 Move the mouse over **Select Files** and then press the left button.

SHORTCUT

Press Alt, F, S

Note: To continue, refer to the next page.

SELECT FILES

Select Files Using Wildcard Characters (Continued)

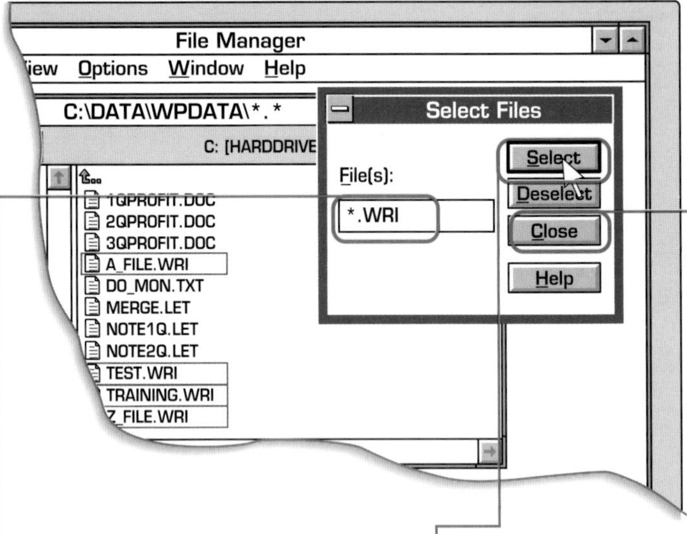

◆ The **Select Files** dialog box appears.

4 Specify the files you want to select by using the wildcard characters (example: type ***.WRI** to select all files with the **WRI** extension).

Note: For more information on wildcards, refer to page 134.

5 Move the mouse ↖ over **Select** and then press the left button.

Tips:

◆ To deselect a single file, press and hold down Ctrl . Still holding down Ctrl , move the mouse over the file and then press the left button.

◆ To deselect all the files, move the mouse over any file and then press the left button.

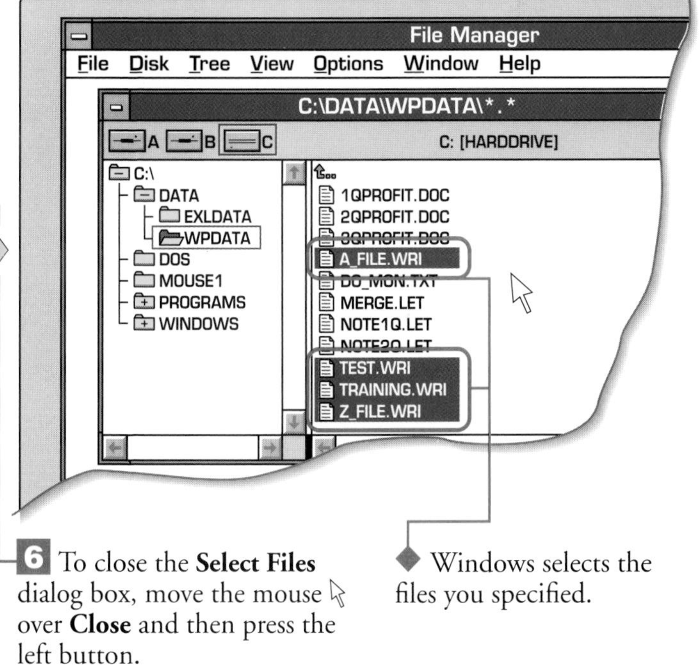

6 To close the **Select Files** dialog box, move the mouse over **Close** and then press the left button.

◆ Windows selects the files you specified.

MOVE OR COPY FILES

You can move or copy files to a different directory.

Move or Copy Files (to a Different Directory)

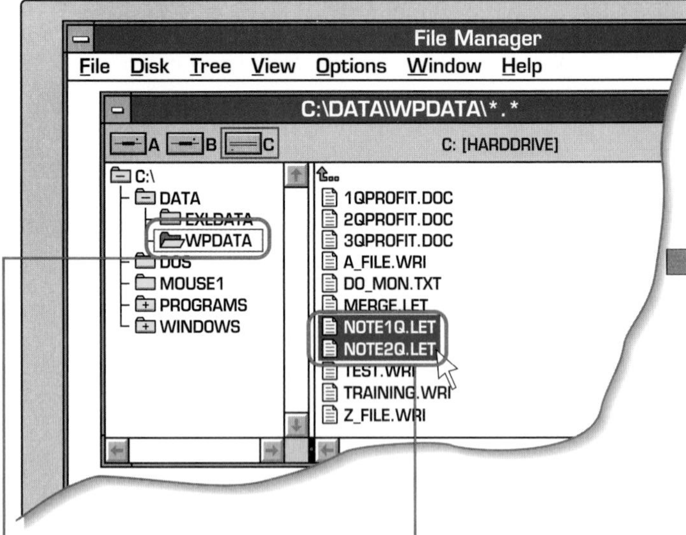

1. Move the mouse over the directory that contains the files you want to move or copy (example: **WPDATA**) and then press the left button.

*Note: To open the **File Manager**, refer to page 76.*

2. Select the files you want to move or copy to a different directory.

Note: To select files, refer to pages 142 to 149.

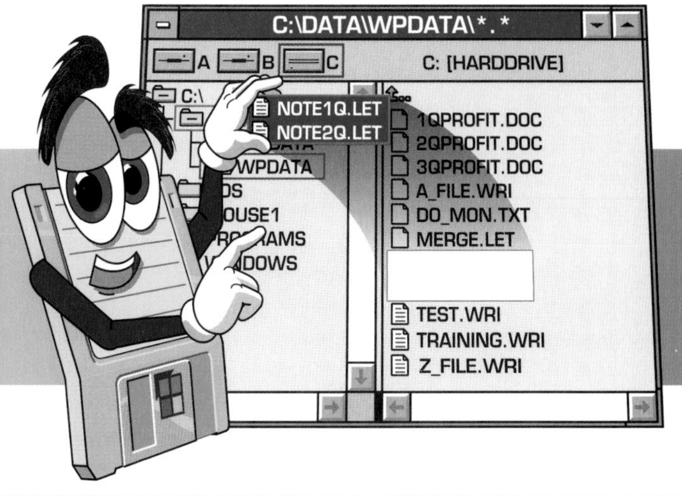

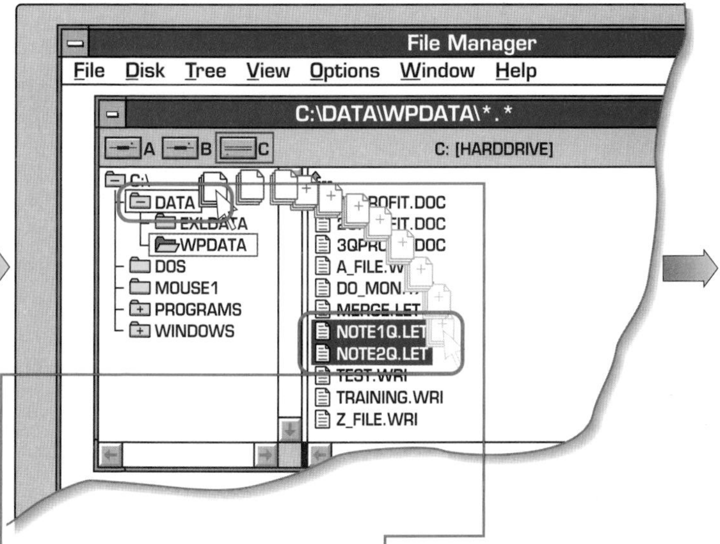

3 Move the mouse over one of the highlighted files and then press and hold down the left button.

4 To copy the files, press and hold down Ctrl. To move the files, do not press Ctrl.

5 Still holding down the button, move the mouse over the directory where you want to move or copy the files (example: **DATA**) and then release the button.

Note: To continue, refer to the next page.

MOVE OR COPY FILES

Move or Copy Files (Continued)

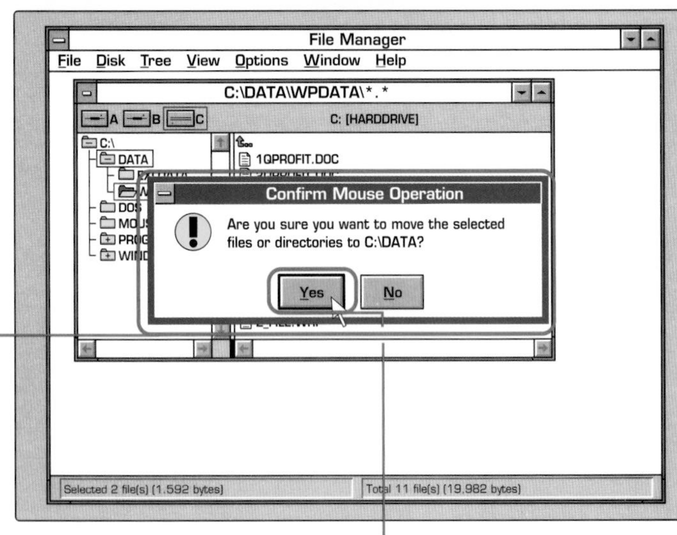

◆ This dialog box offers you a final chance to cancel the move or copy.

6 To move or copy the files, move the mouse ⇖ over **Yes** and then press the left button.

*Note: To cancel the move or copy, move the mouse ⇖ over **No** and then press the left button.*

COPY FILES

The Copy command places exact copies of your files in a new location. Windows does not delete the original files.

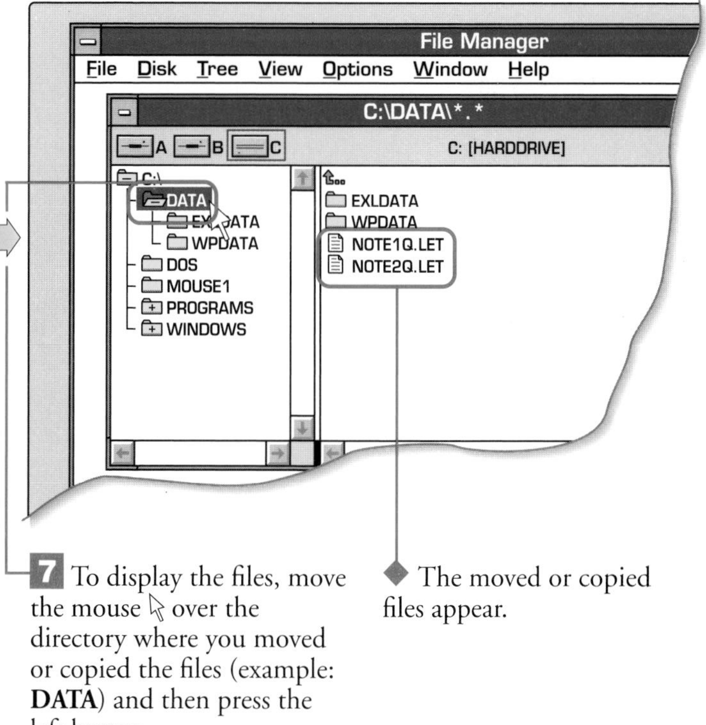

7 To display the files, move the mouse over the directory where you moved or copied the files (example: **DATA**) and then press the left button.

◆ The moved or copied files appear.

MOVE OR COPY FILES

Move or Copy Files (to a Different Drive)

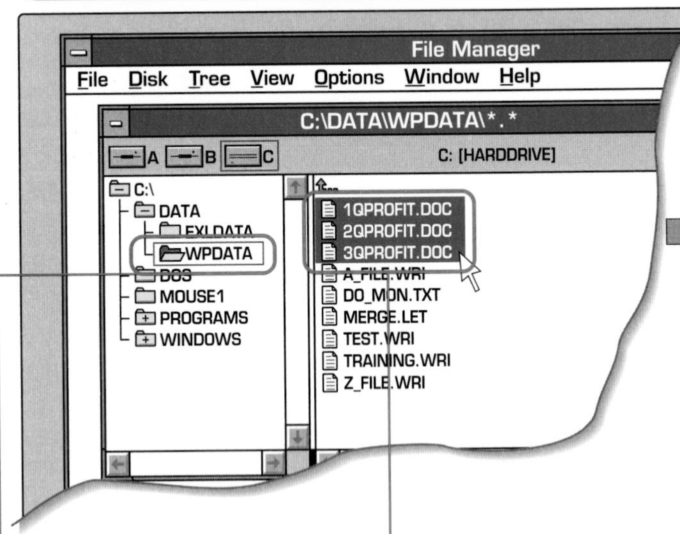

1 Move the mouse over the directory that contains the files you want to move or copy (example: **WPDATA**) and then press the left button.

*Note: To open the **File Manager**, refer to page 76.*

2 Select the files you want to move or copy to a different drive.

Note: To select files, refer to pages 142 to 149.

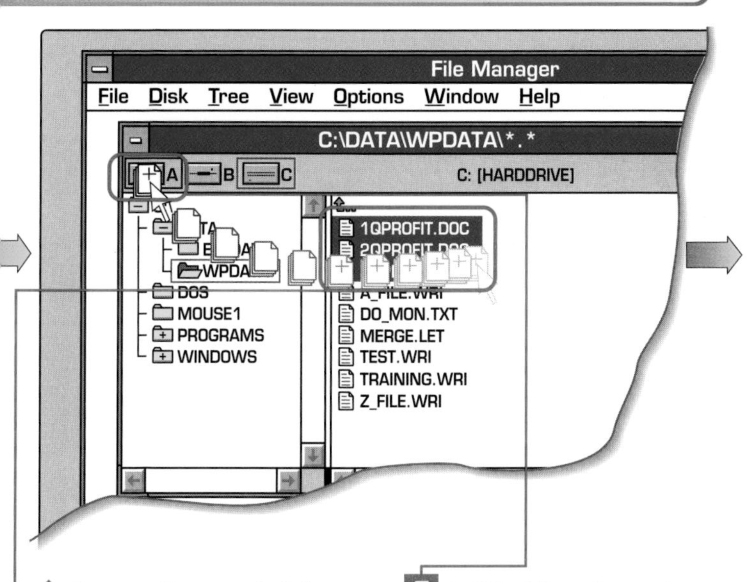

◆ Insert a formatted diskette in the drive where you want to move or copy the files.

3 Move the mouse ↖ over one of the highlighted files and then press and hold down the left button.

4 To move the files, press and hold down Alt . To copy the files, do not press Alt .

5 Still holding down the button, move the mouse ↖ over the drive where you want to move or copy the files (example: **drive A**) and then release the button.

Note: To continue, refer to the next page.

Move or Copy Files (Continued)

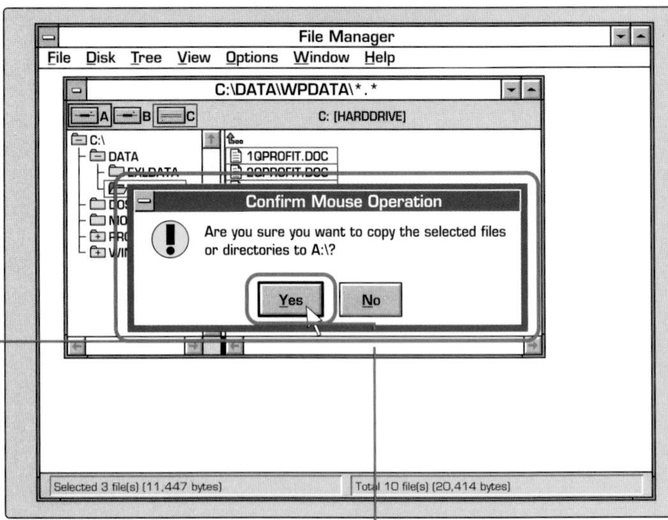

◆ Windows offers you a final chance to cancel the move or copy.

6 To move or copy the files, move the mouse over **Yes** and then press the left button.

*Note: To cancel the move or copy, move the mouse over **No** and then press the left button.*

COPY FILES

The Copy command places exact copies of your files in a new location. Windows does not delete the original files.

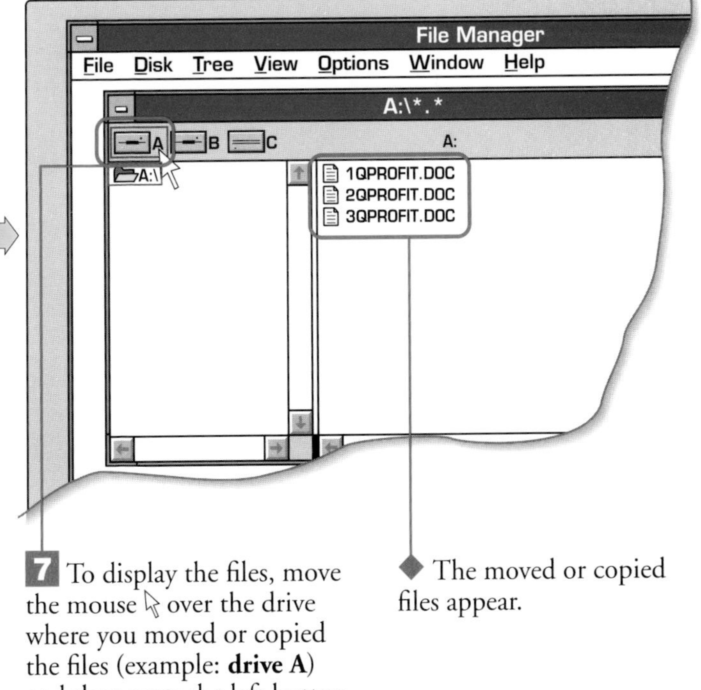

7 To display the files, move the mouse over the drive where you moved or copied the files (example: **drive A**) and then press the left button.

◆ The moved or copied files appear.

RENAME A FILE

Rename a File

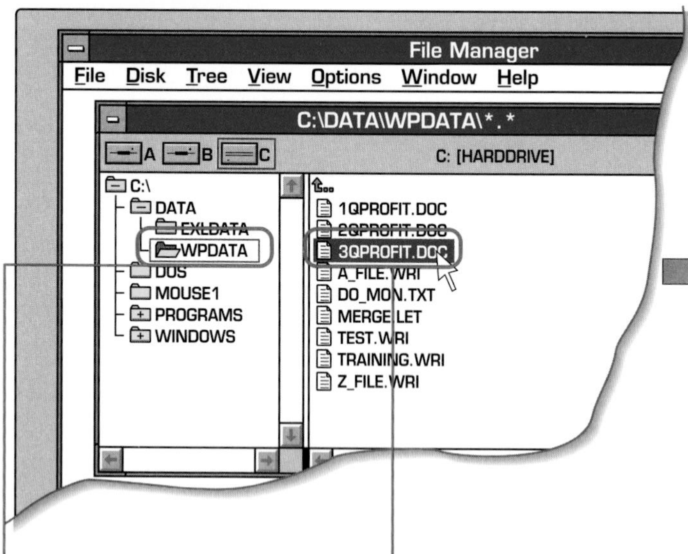

1 Move the mouse ↖ over the directory that contains the file you want to rename (example: **WPDATA**) and then press the left button.

*Note: To open the **File Manager**, refer to page 76.*

2 To select the file you want to rename, move the mouse ↖ over the file (example: **3QPROFIT.DOC**) and then press the left button.

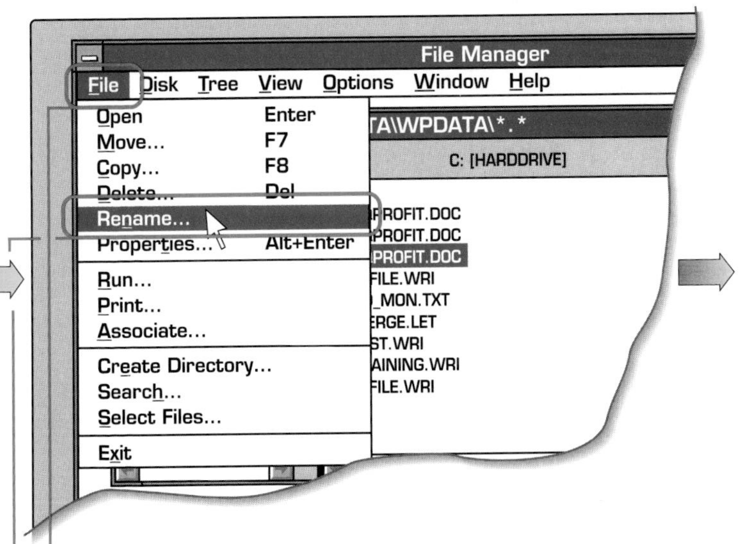

3 Move the mouse over **File** and then press the left button.

4 Move the mouse over **Rename** and then press the left button.

Note: To continue, refer to the next page.

RENAME A FILE

Rename a File (Continued)

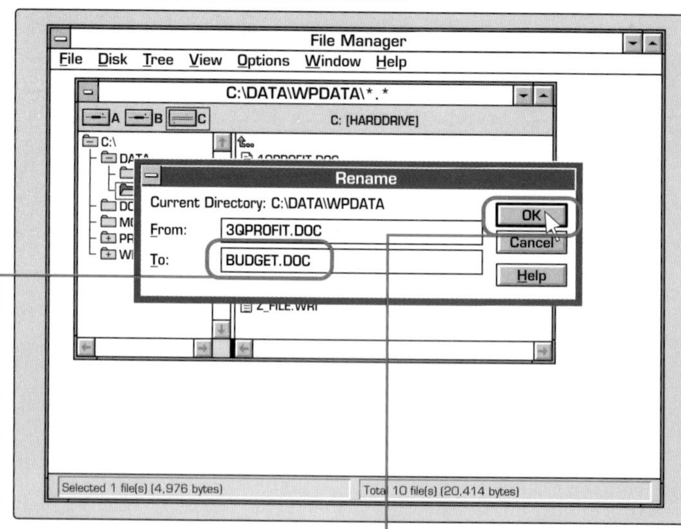

◆ The **Rename** dialog box appears.

5 Type a new name for the file (example: **BUDGET.DOC**).

6 Move the mouse over **OK** and then press the left button.

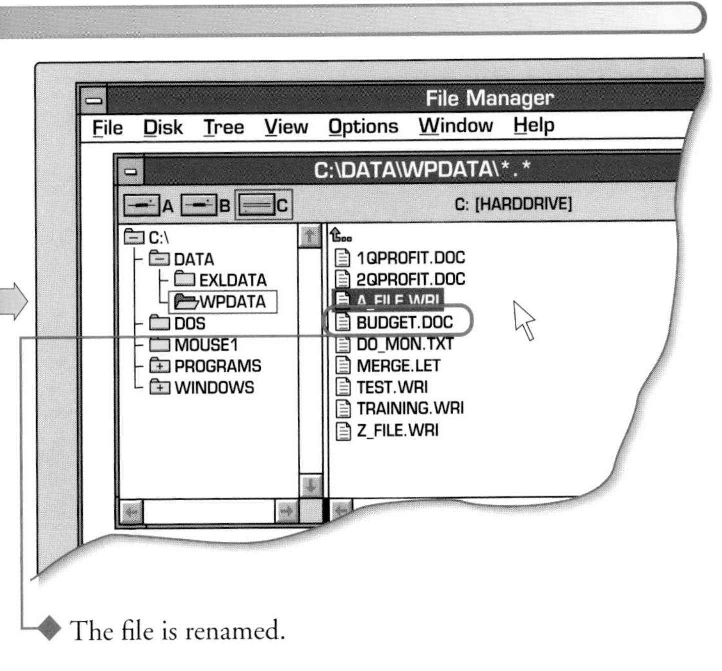

◆ The file is renamed.

DELETE FILES

Delete Files

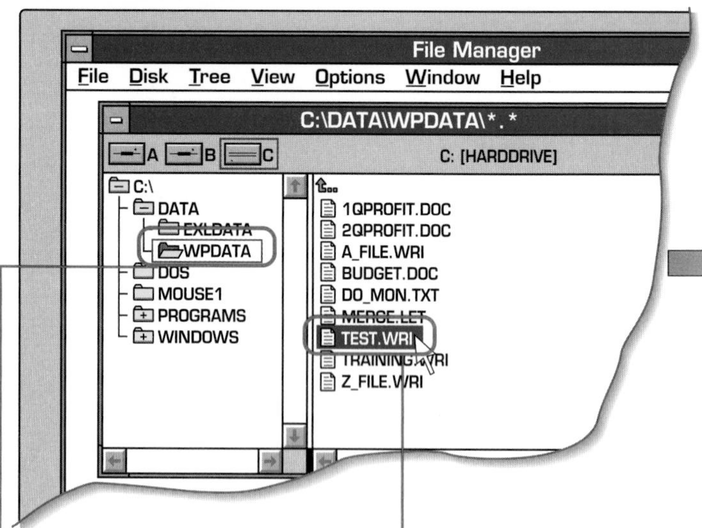

1 Move the mouse over the directory that contains the file(s) you want to delete (example: **WPDATA**) and then press the left button.

*Note: To open the **File Manager**, refer to page 76.*

2 Select the file(s) you want to delete (example: **TEST.WRI**).

Note: To select files, refer to pages 142 to 149.

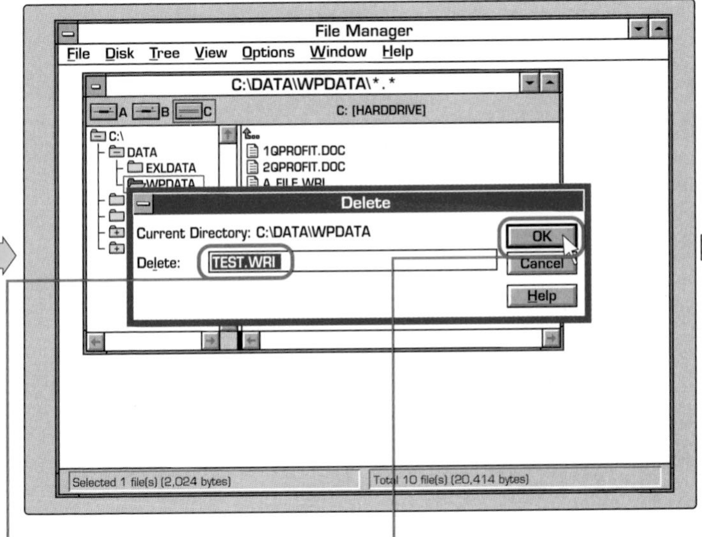

3 Press Delete and the **Delete** dialog box appears.

◆ Windows displays the name(s) of the file(s) it will delete (example: **TEST.WRI**).

4 Move the mouse over **OK** and then press the left button.

Note: To continue, refer to the next page.

DELETE FILES

Delete Files (Continued)

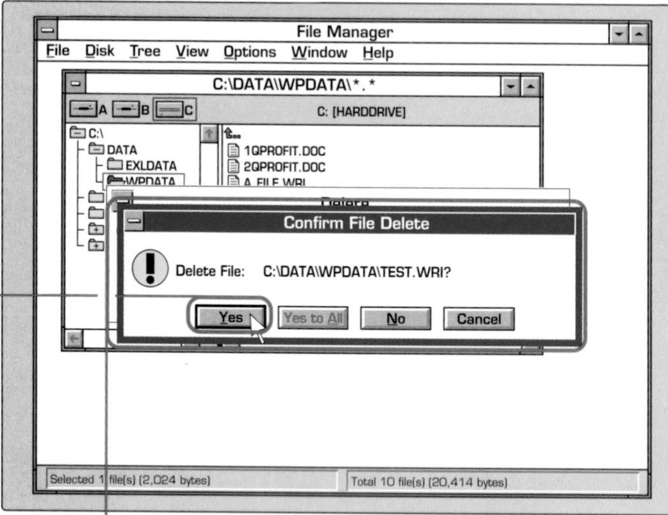

◆ Windows offers you a final chance to cancel the deletion.

5 To delete the file, move the mouse over **Yes** and then press the left button.

Note: If you do not want to delete the file, move the mouse over ***No*** *and then press the left button.*

6 If you selected more than one file in step **2**, repeat step **5** until you have deleted all the files.

or

To delete all the files at the same time, move the mouse over **Yes to All** and then press the left button.

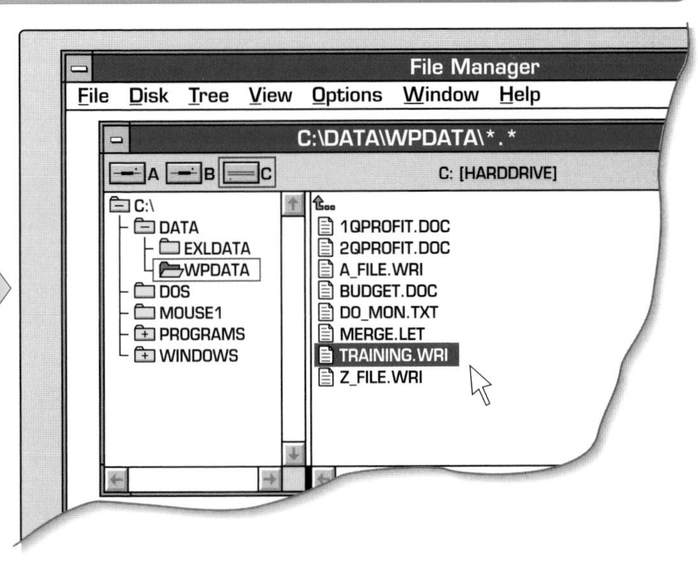

◆ The file is deleted.

DISKETTES

You can protect the files stored on your computer by copying them to diskettes. These will serve as backup copies if your hard drive fails or you accidentally erase important files.

TRANSFER FILES TO ANOTHER COMPUTER

You can use diskettes to transfer files from one computer to another.

FREE HARD DISK SPACE

You can copy old or rarely used files to diskettes. Remove these files from your hard drive to free disk space.

DISKETTES

5.25 Inch Diskettes

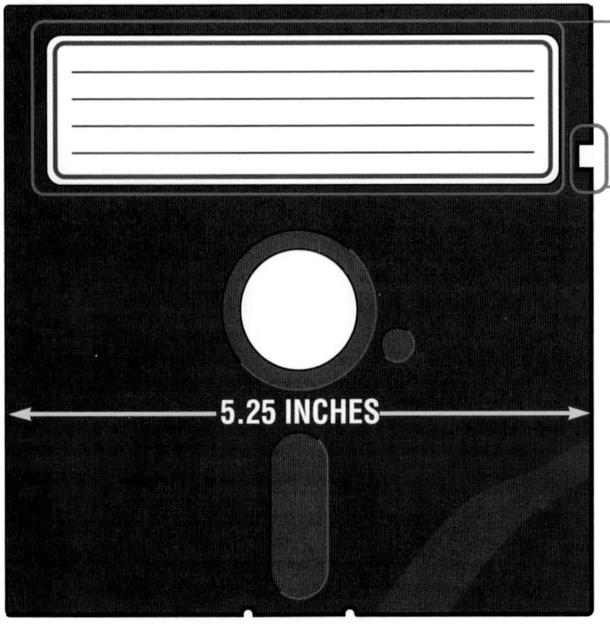

3.5 Inch Diskettes

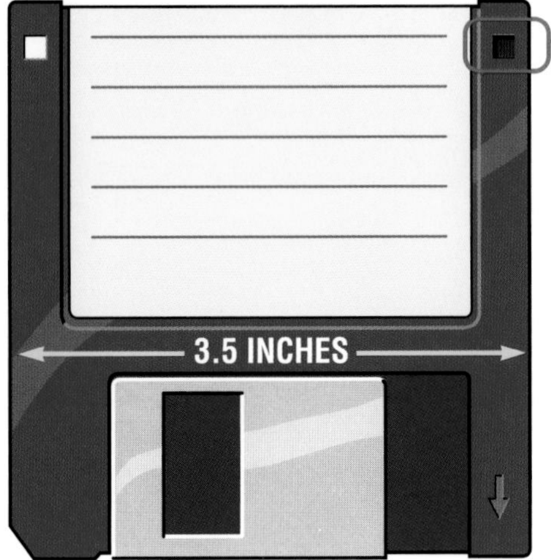

◆ Most diskettes provide you with a label to describe their contents. Use a soft-tipped felt marker to write on the label. A pen or pencil may damage the diskette.

◆ You can prevent erasing and recording information on this diskette by placing a small sticker over the "Write-Protect" notch.

Not Write-Protected

Write-Protected

◆ You can prevent erasing and recording information on this diskette by moving the tab to the "Write-Protected" position.

Not Write-Protected

Write-Protected

DISKETTE CAPACITY

Diskette Capacity

3.5 and 5.25 inch diskettes offer two types of storage capacities.

◆ A high-density diskette can store more information than a double-density diskette of the same size.

◆ High-density 3.5 inch diskettes usually display the HD symbol. They also have two holes at the top of the diskette. Double-density diskettes have only one hole.

Type	Capacity
Double-density	720K
High-density	1.44MB

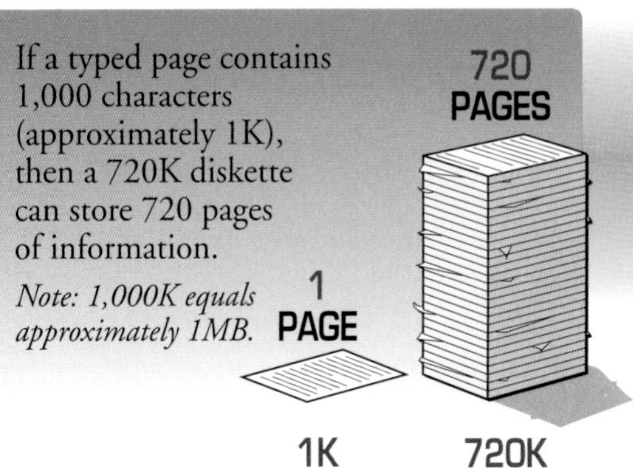

If a typed page contains 1,000 characters (approximately 1K), then a 720K diskette can store 720 pages of information.

Note: 1,000K equals approximately 1MB.

◆ Double-density 5.25 inch diskettes are usually labeled. They also display a double ring. High-density diskettes do not display a double ring.

Type	Capacity
Double-density	360K
High-density	1.2MB

FORMAT A DISK

Format a Disk

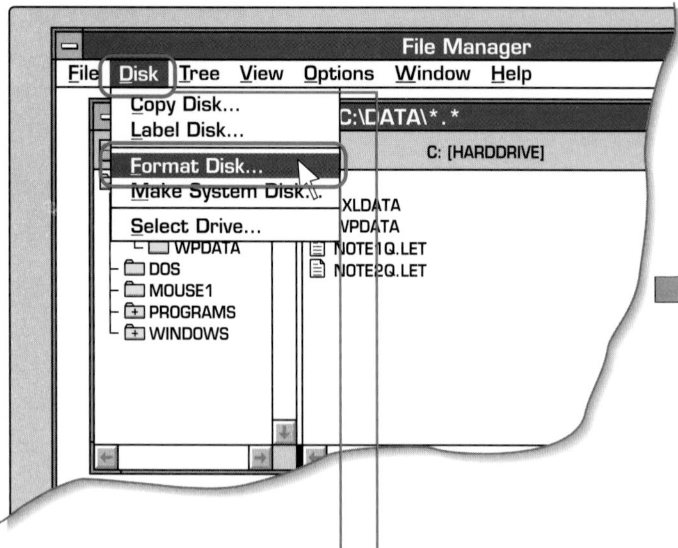

1 Insert the disk you want to format into a drive (example: **Drive B:**).

*Note: To open the **File Manager**, refer to page 76.*

2 Move the mouse ↖ over **Disk** and then press the left button.

3 Move the mouse ↖ over **Format Disk** and then press the left button.

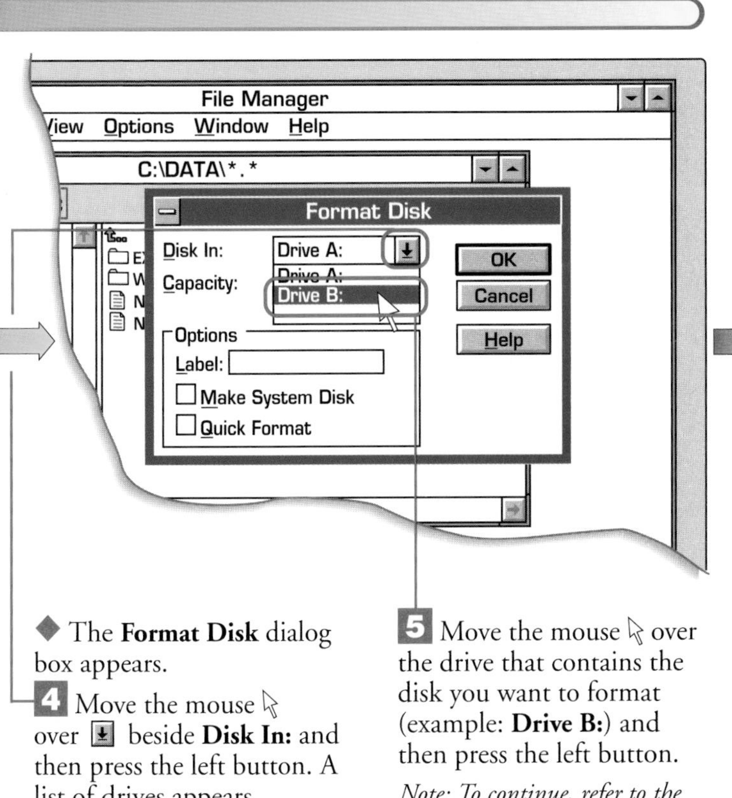

◆ The **Format Disk** dialog box appears.

4 Move the mouse over ⬇ beside **Disk In:** and then press the left button. A list of drives appears.

5 Move the mouse over the drive that contains the disk you want to format (example: **Drive B:**) and then press the left button.

Note: To continue, refer to the next page.

Format a Disk (Continued)

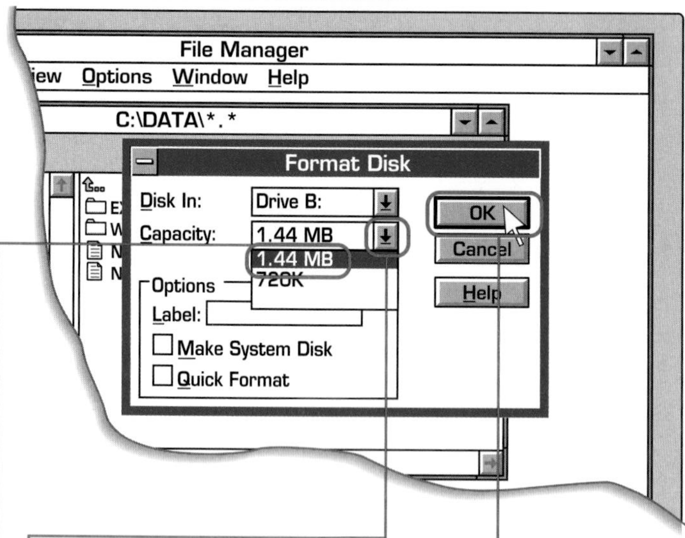

6 Move the mouse over ⬇ beside **Capacity:** and then press the left button. A list of capacities appears.

7 Move the mouse over the storage capacity of the disk you are about to format (example: **1.44 MB**) and then press the left button.

Note: For information on disk storage capacity, refer to page 170.

8 Move the mouse over **OK** and then press the left button.

The Format command erases all the information on your diskette. Do not format a diskette containing information you want to keep.

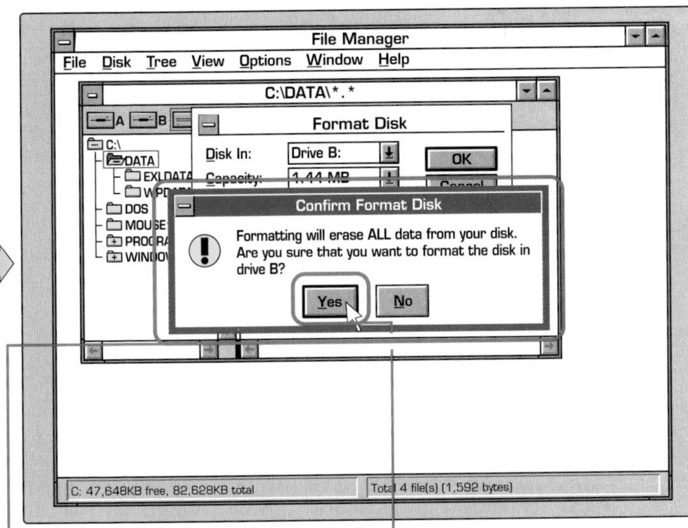

◆ This dialog box offers you a final chance to cancel the format.

*Note: To cancel the format, move the mouse over **No** and then press the left button.*

9 To format the disk, move the mouse over **Yes** and then press the left button.

Note: To continue, refer to the next page.

FORMAT A DISK

Format a Disk (Continued)

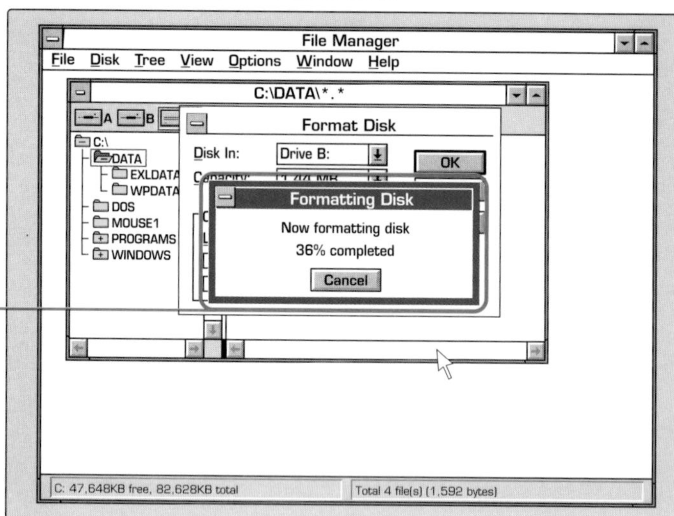

◆ A dialog box appears displaying the progress of the format.

Tip:

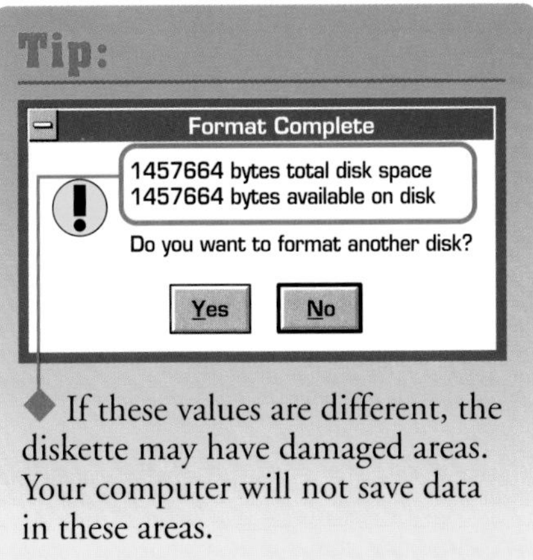

◆ If these values are different, the diskette may have damaged areas. Your computer will not save data in these areas.

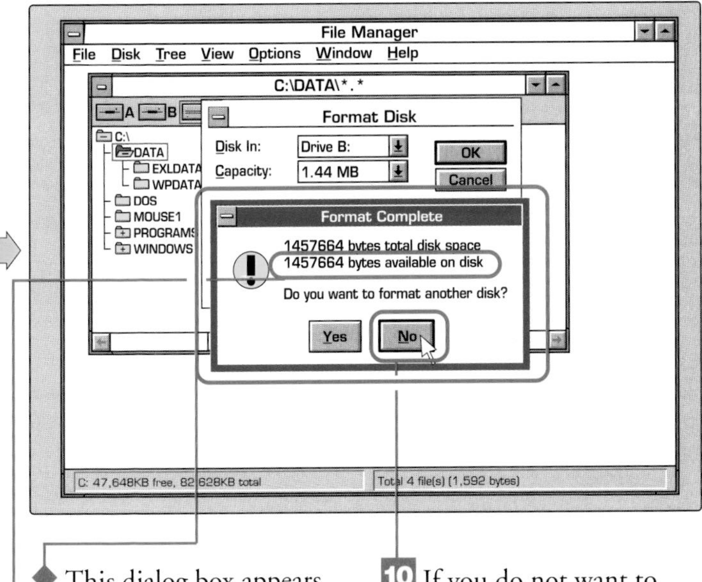

◆ This dialog box appears when the format is complete.

◆ The total bytes available on the disk are displayed.

10 If you do not want to format another disk, move the mouse ⇖ over **No** and then press the left button.

Note: To format another disk, move the mouse ⇖ over ***Yes*** *and then press the left button.*

COPY A DISK

Copy a Disk

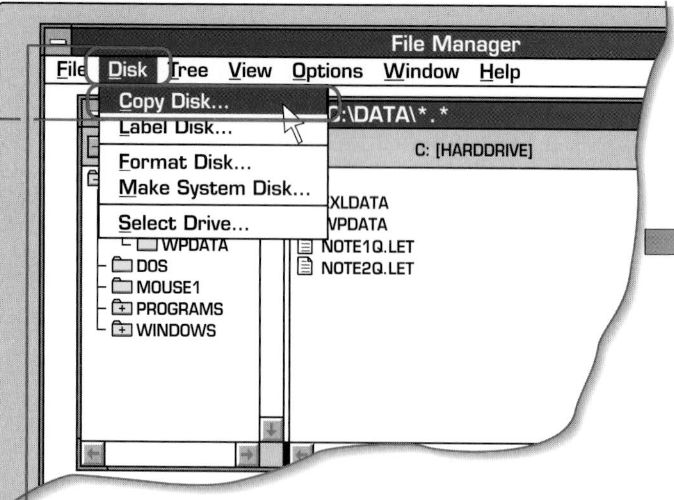

1 Move the mouse over **Disk** and then press the left button.

2 Move the mouse over **Copy Disk** and then press the left button.

*Note: To open the **File Manager**, refer to page 76.*

Note: The source and destination diskettes must be the same size and capacity.

Destination Disk

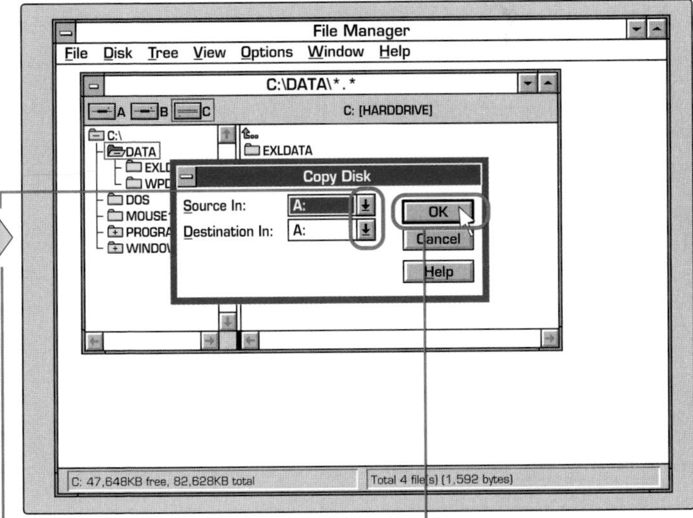

◆ The **Copy Disk** dialog box appears only if your computer has two disk drives (**A:** and **B:**).

◆ To change the source or destination drive, move the mouse ⇖ over an arrow ⬇ and then press the left button. Move the mouse ⇖ over the drive you want to use and then press the left button.

3 Move the mouse ⇖ over **OK** and then press the left button.

Note: To continue, refer to the next page.

Copy a Disk (Continued)

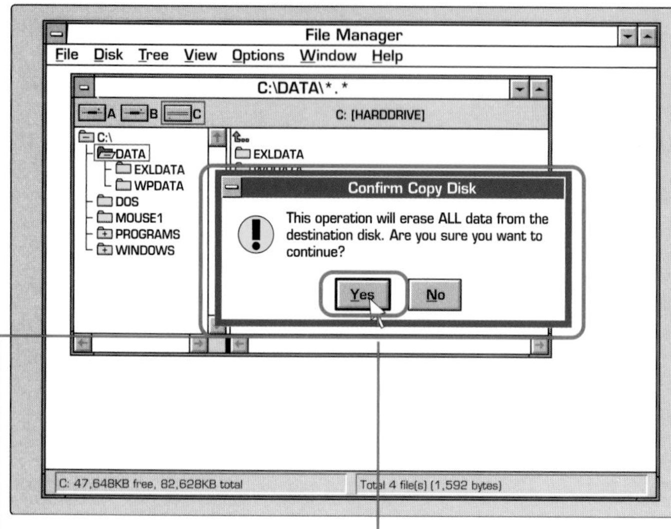

◆ This dialog box offers you a final chance to cancel the copy.

4 To copy the disk, move the mouse over **Yes** and then press the left button.

Note: To cancel the copy, move the mouse over ***No*** *and then press the left button.*

When using the Copy Disk command, make sure the destination diskette does not contain information you want to keep. The Copy Disk command will permanently erase the data from the disk.

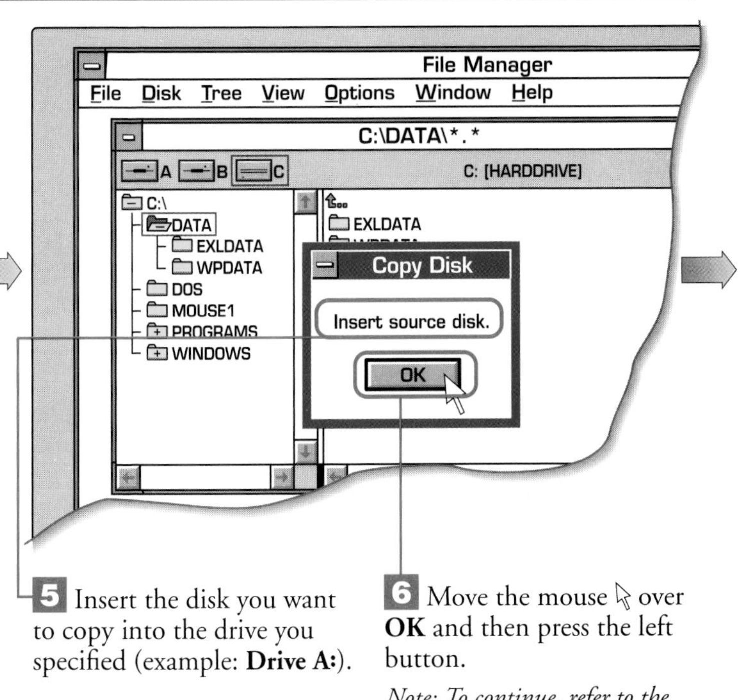

5 Insert the disk you want to copy into the drive you specified (example: **Drive A:**).

6 Move the mouse over **OK** and then press the left button.

Note: To continue, refer to the next page.

COPY A DISK

Copy a Disk (Continued)

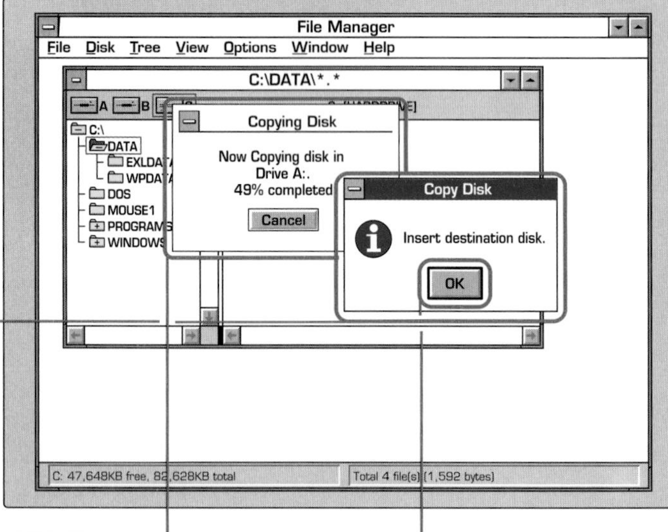

◆ This dialog box appears displaying the progress of the copy.

7 When this dialog box appears, remove the source disk from the drive.

8 Insert the destination disk into the drive you specified (example: **Drive A:**).

9 Move the mouse over **OK** and then press the left button.

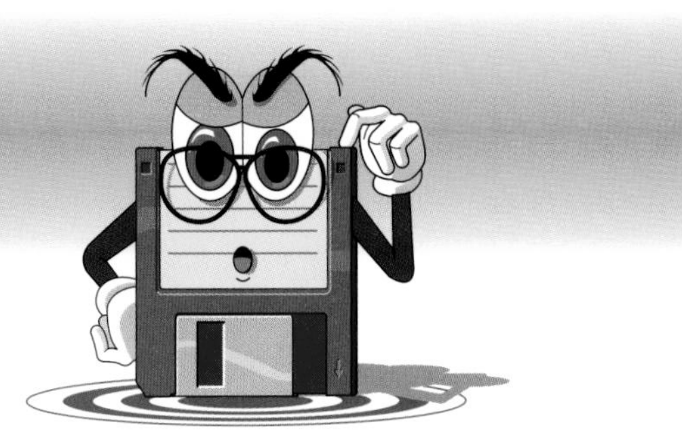

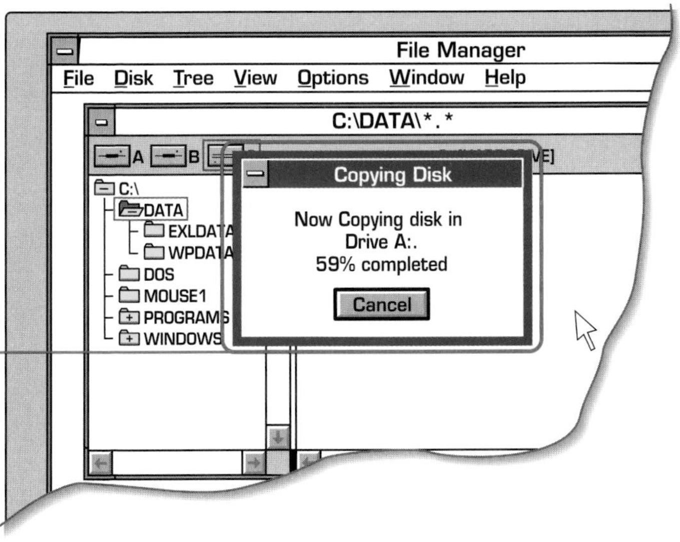
File Manager
File Disk Tree View Options Window Help
C:\DATA*.*
Copying Disk
Now Copying disk in
Drive A:.
59% completed
Cancel
C:\
DATA
DOS
MOUSE1

◆ This dialog box appears displaying the progress of the copy. It disappears when the copy is complete.

START WRITE

Start Write

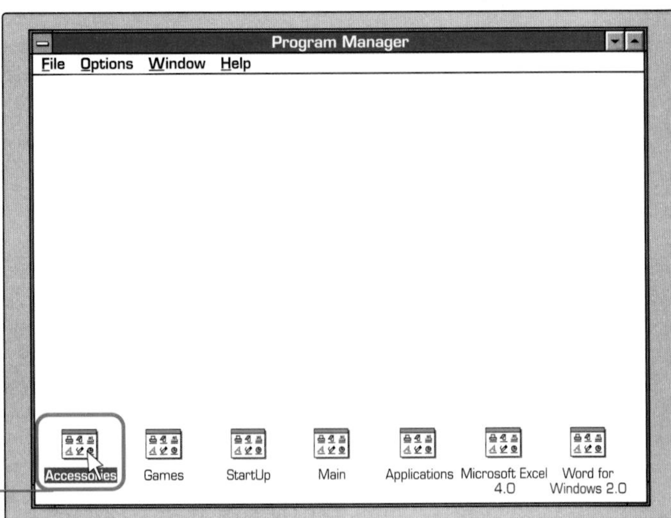

1 To open the **Accessories** group window, move the mouse over its icon and then quickly press the left button twice.

The Write program is a simple word processor that enables you to write letters, memos and reports.

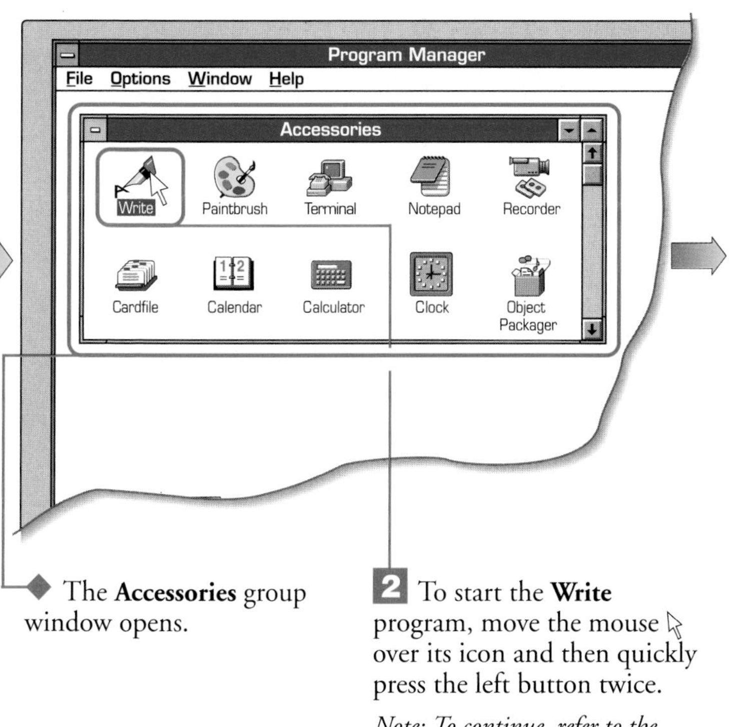

◆ The **Accessories** group window opens.

2 To start the **Write** program, move the mouse over its icon and then quickly press the left button twice.

Note: To continue, refer to the next page.

START WRITE

Start Write (Continued)

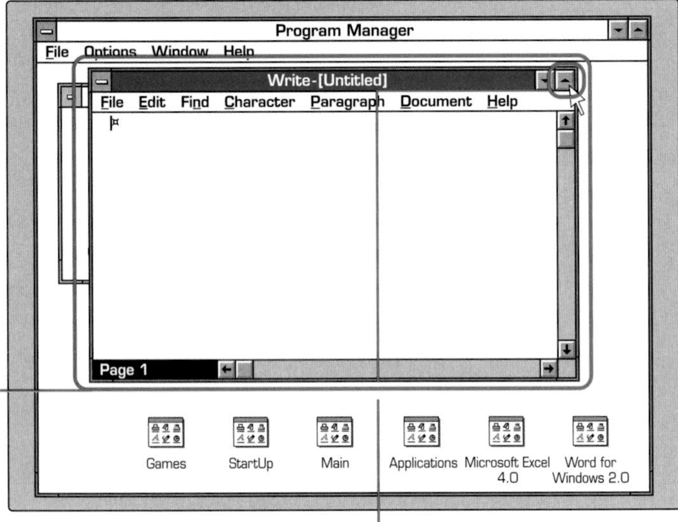

◆ The **Write** window opens, displaying a new document.

3 To enlarge the **Write** window to fill your entire screen, move the mouse ⇖ over its **Maximize** button and then press the left button.

When using a word processor to type a
letter, the text automatically wraps to the
next line as you type.

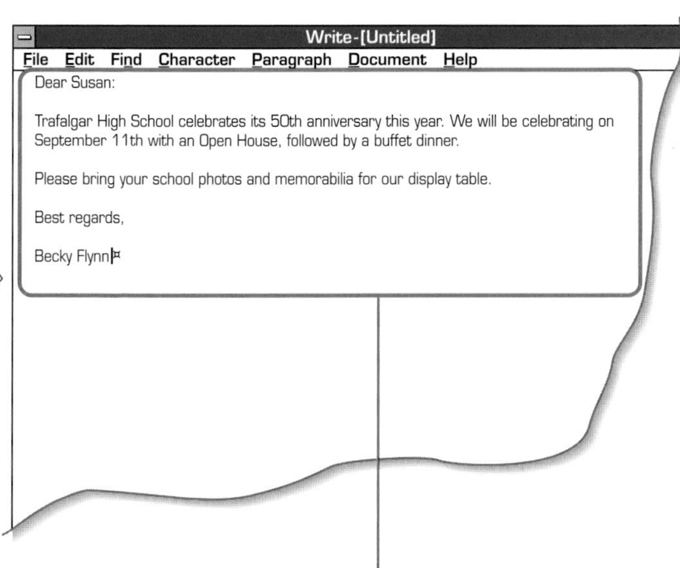

◆ The flashing line on your screen is called the insertion point. This indicates where the text you type will appear.

4 Type the text.

◆ Press **Enter** only when you want to start a new line or paragraph.

MOVE WITHIN WRITE

Move Within Write (Using the Mouse)

Write-[Untitled]

File Edit Find Character Paragraph Document H

Dear Susan:

Trafalgar High School celebrates its 50th anniversary this year.
September 11th with an Open House, followed by a buffet dinn

Please bring your school photos and memorabilia for our displ

Best regards,

Becky Flynn

1 Position the mouse I where you want to move the insertion point.

Note: The insertion point indicates where the text you type will appear.

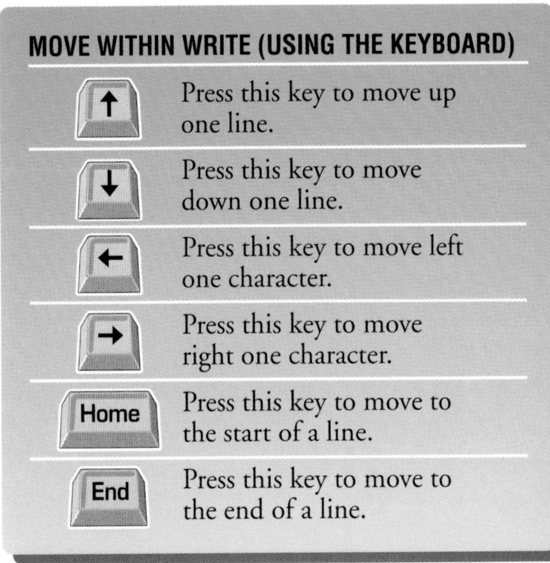

MOVE WITHIN WRITE (USING THE KEYBOARD)

↑	Press this key to move up one line.
↓	Press this key to move down one line.
←	Press this key to move left one character.
→	Press this key to move right one character.
Home	Press this key to move to the start of a line.
End	Press this key to move to the end of a line.

2 Press the left button and the insertion point moves to the new location.

SELECT TEXT

Select any Amount of Text

Write - [Untitled]

File Edit Find Character Paragraph Document Help

Dear Susan:

Trafalgar High School celebrates its 50th anniversary this year. We will September 11th with an Open House, followed by a buffet dinner.

Please bring your school photos and memorabilia for our display table.

Best regards,

Becky Flynn ¤

1 Move the mouse I to the left of the first character you want to select.

To perform a command on a section of text, you must first select the text. This highlights (isolates) the text so Write knows to work with only those characters.

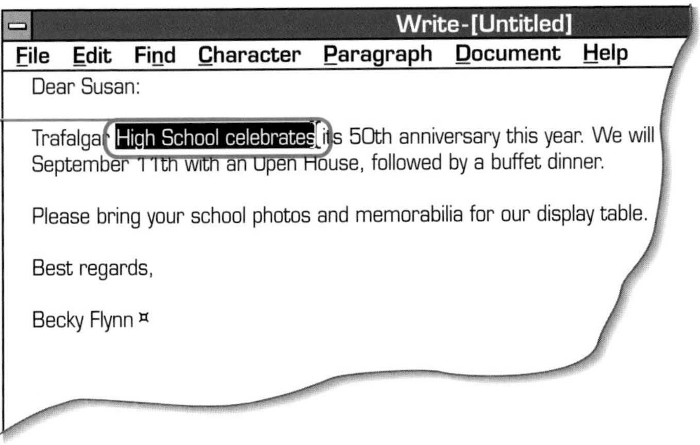

Write-[Untitled]
File Edit Find Character Paragraph Document Help
Dear Susan:

Trafalgar High School celebrates its 50th anniversary this year. We will September 11th with an Open House, followed by a buffet dinner.

Please bring your school photos and memorabilia for our display table.

Best regards,

Becky Flynn

2 To select the text, press and hold down the left button and then drag the mouse I until you highlight the text.

3 Release the button.

◆ To cancel a text selection, press the left button.

SAVE A DOCUMENT

Save a Document

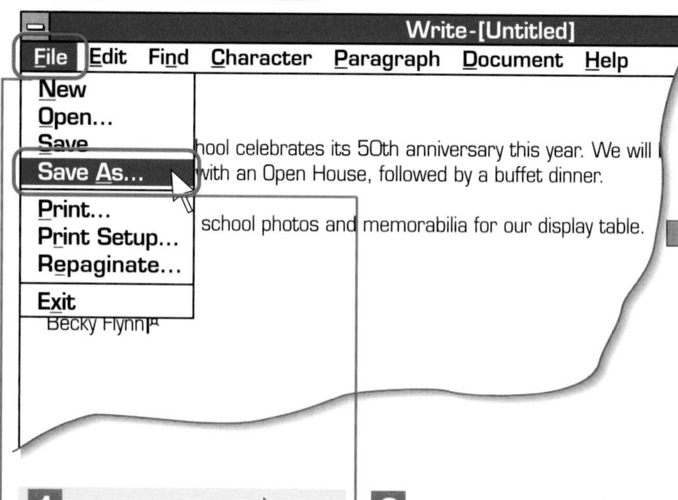

1 Move the mouse over **File** and then press the left button.

2 Move the mouse over **Save As** and then press the left button.

When you finish working on your document, save it before starting something else or exiting Write. This permanently stores your document for future use.

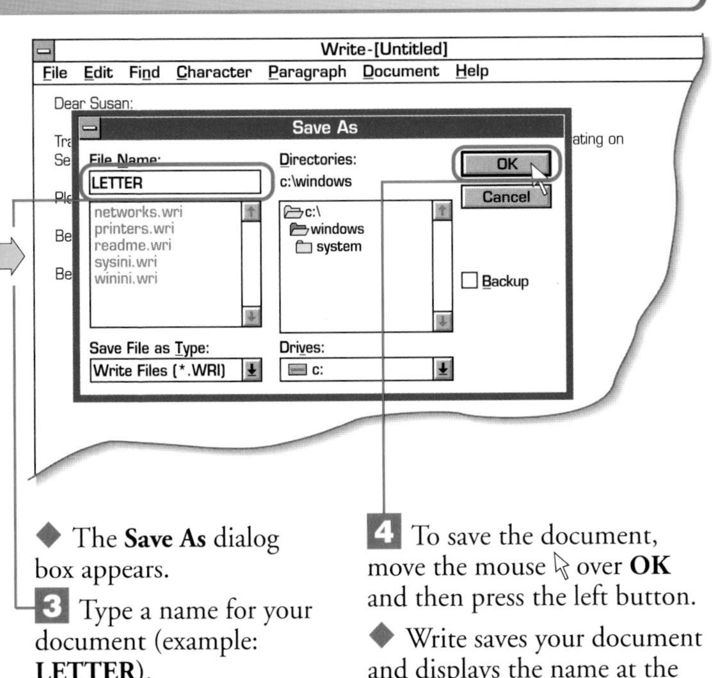

◆ The **Save As** dialog box appears.

3 Type a name for your document (example: **LETTER**).

4 To save the document, move the mouse over **OK** and then press the left button.

◆ Write saves your document and displays the name at the top of your screen (example: **Write-LETTER.WRI**).

EXIT WRITE

Exiting Write will return you to the Program Manager.

Exit Write

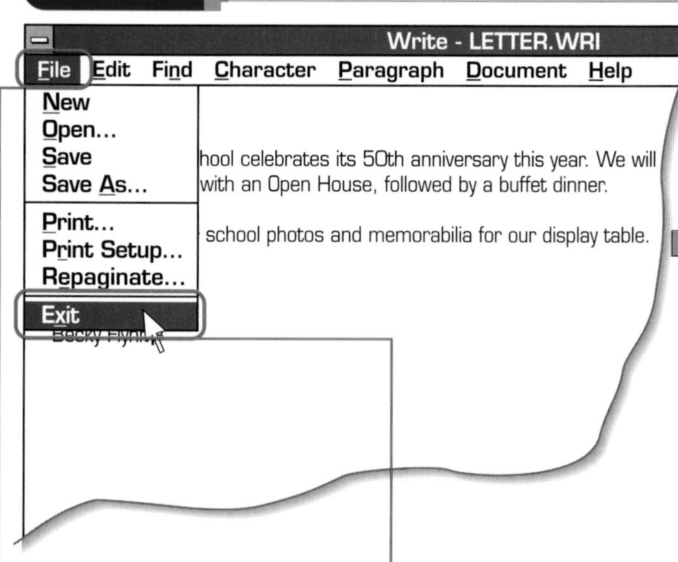

1 Move the mouse ⇖ over **File** and then press the left button.

2 Move the mouse ⇖ over **Exit** and then press the left button.

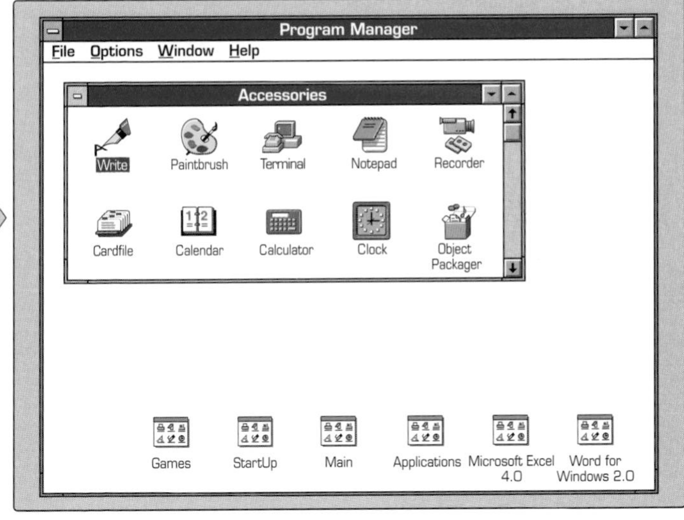

◆ The **Program Manager** window appears.

Note: To restart ***Write****, refer to page 184.*

OPEN A DOCUMENT

Open a Document

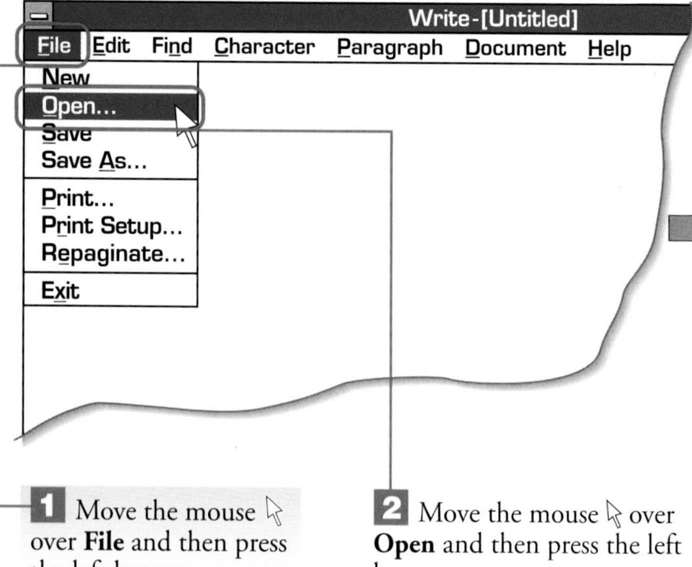

1 Move the mouse over **File** and then press the left button.

2 Move the mouse over **Open** and then press the left button.

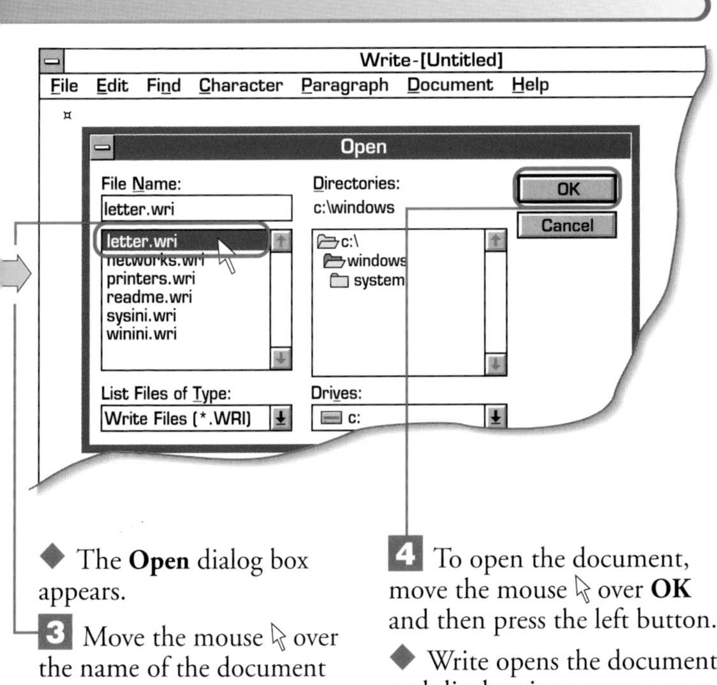

◆ The **Open** dialog box appears.

3 Move the mouse over the name of the document you want to open (example: **letter.wri**) and then press the left button.

4 To open the document, move the mouse over **OK** and then press the left button.

◆ Write opens the document and displays it on your screen.

INSERT TEXT

Insert Text

Write - LETTER.WRI

File Edit Find Character Paragraph Document Help

Dear Susan:

Trafalgar High School celebrates its 50th anniversary this year. We will be
September 11th with an Open House, followed by a buffet dinner.

Please bring your school photos and memorabilia for our display table.

Best regards,

Becky Flynn

1 Move the mouse I where you want to insert the new text and then press the left button.

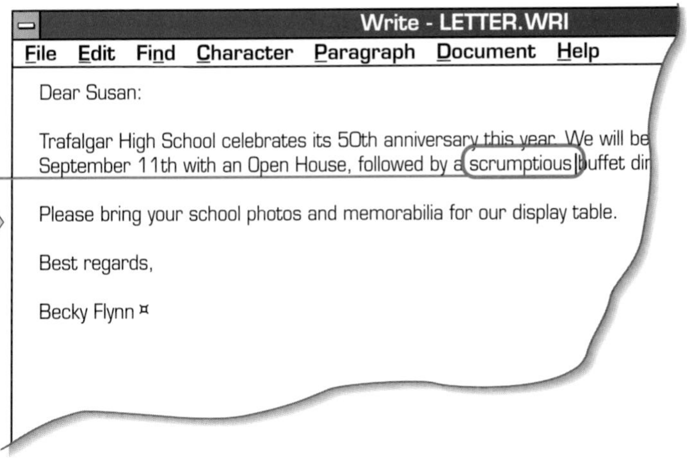

Write - LETTER.WRI

File Edit Find Character Paragraph Document Help

Dear Susan:

Trafalgar High School celebrates its 50th anniversary this year. We will be
September 11th with an Open House, followed by a scrumptious buffet dir

Please bring your school photos and memorabilia for our display table.

Best regards,

Becky Flynn ¤

2 Type the text you want to insert (example: **scrumptious**).

3 To insert a blank space, press the **Spacebar**.

Note: The words to the right of the inserted text are pushed forward.

DELETE TEXT

Delete Text

Write - LETTER.WRI

File Edit Find Character Paragraph Document Help

Dear Susan:

Trafalgar High School celebrates its 50th anniversary this year. We will be
September 11th with an Open House, followed by a scrumptious buffet di

Please bring your school photos and memorabilia for our display table.

Best regards,

Becky Flynn ¤

1 Select the text you want to delete (example: **scrumptious**).

Note: To select text, refer to page 190.

DELETE A CHARACTER

1 Position the insertion point to the left of the character you want to delete.

2 Press Delete to remove the character.

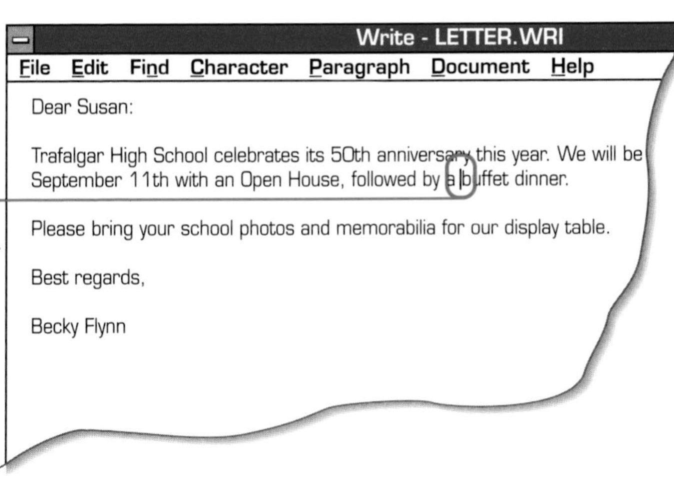

2 Press Delete to remove the text.

Move Text

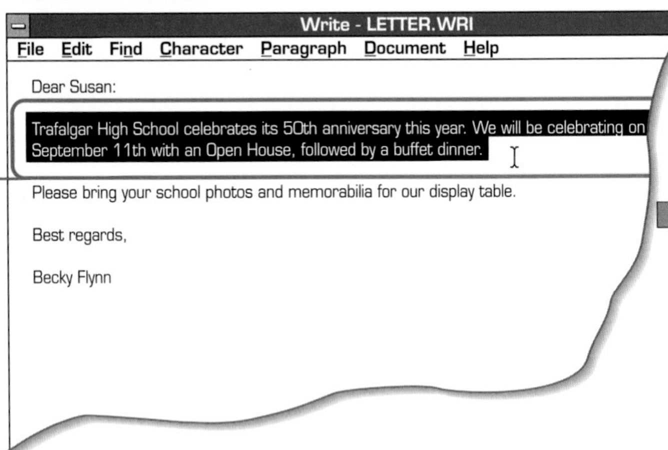

1 Select the text you want to move.

Note: To select text, refer to page 190.

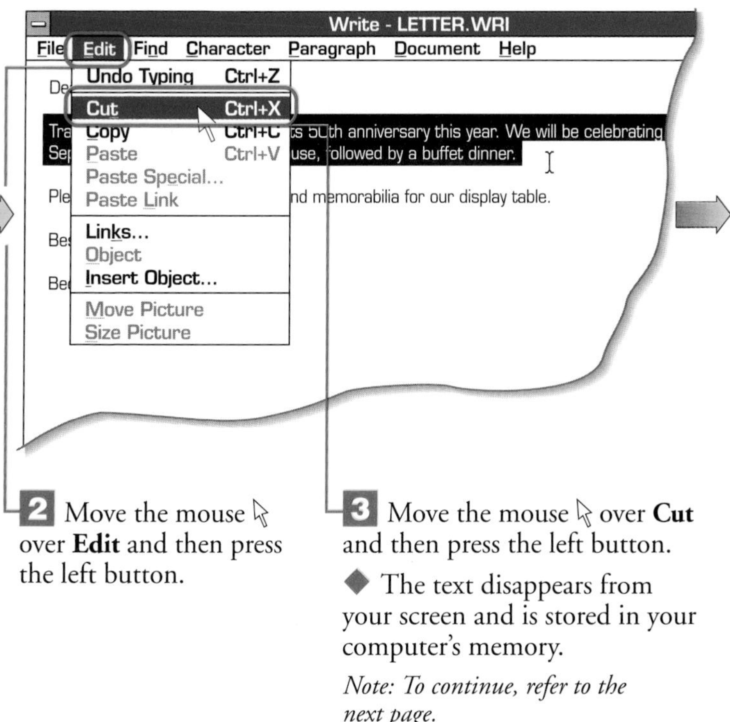

2 Move the mouse over **Edit** and then press the left button.

3 Move the mouse over **Cut** and then press the left button.

◆ The text disappears from your screen and is stored in your computer's memory.

Note: To continue, refer to the next page.

MOVE TEXT

Move Text (Continued)

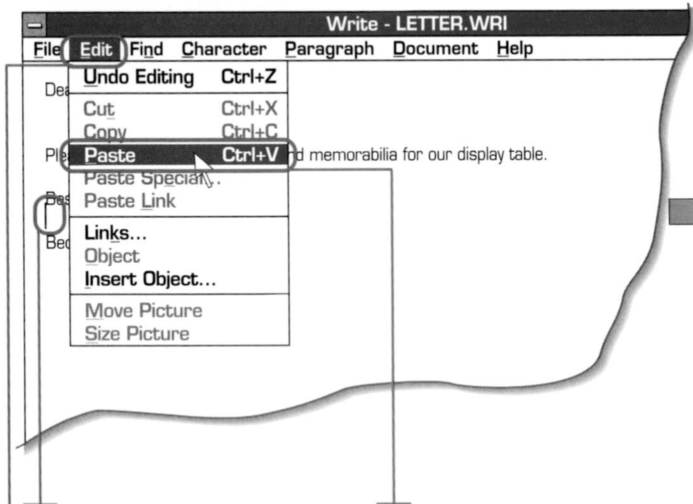

4 Move the mouse I where you want the text to appear and then press the left button.

5 Move the mouse over **Edit** and then press the left button.

6 Move the mouse over **Paste** and then press the left button.

COPY TEXT

You can copy text from one location in your document to another. Write copies the text and pastes the copy in a new location. The original text remains in its place.

To copy text:

◆ Repeat steps 1 to 6 starting on page 202, except select **Copy** in step 3.

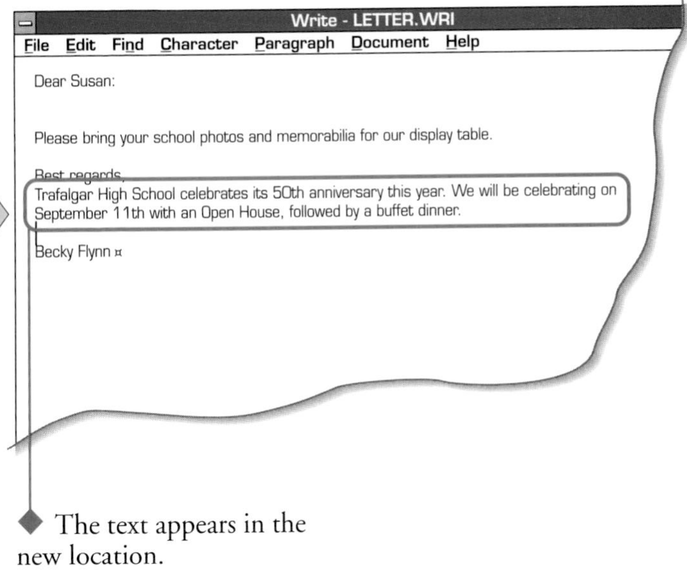

◆ The text appears in the new location.

PRINT A FILE

Print a File

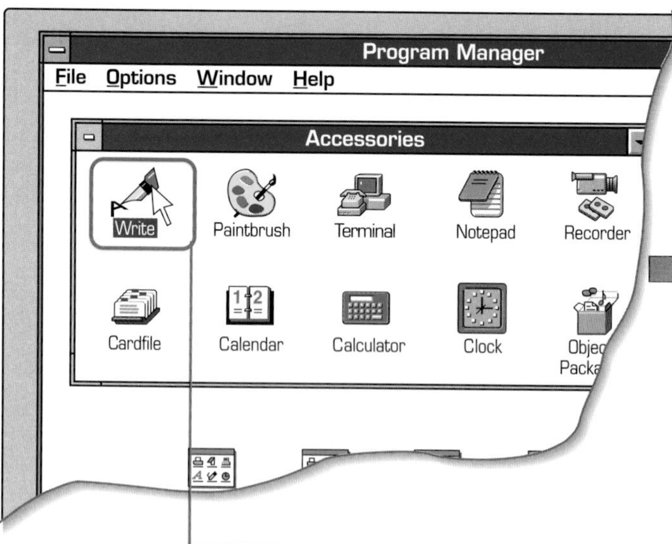

1 Start the application containing the document you want to print (example: **Write**).

◆ To start the **Write** application, move the mouse over its icon and then quickly press the left button twice.

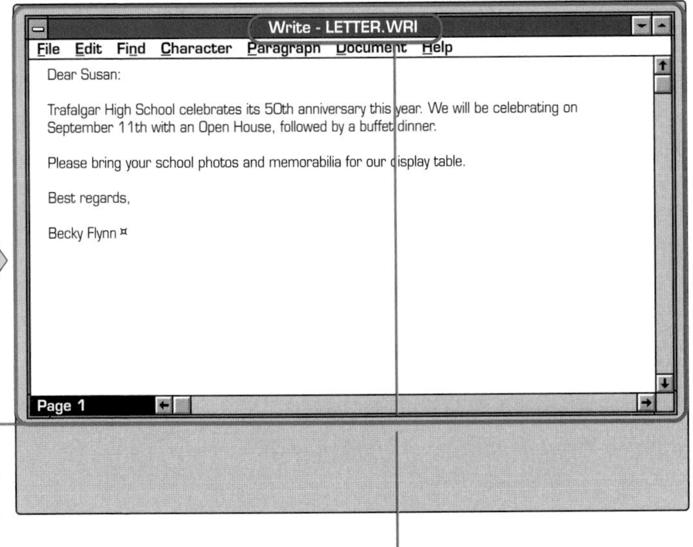

◆ The **Write** window opens.

2 Move and size the window as shown above.

Note: To move a window, refer to page 20. To size a window, refer to page 22.

3 Open the document you want to print (example: **LETTER.WRI**). To open a document, refer to page 196.

Note: To continue, refer to the next page.

PRINT A FILE

Print a File (Continued)

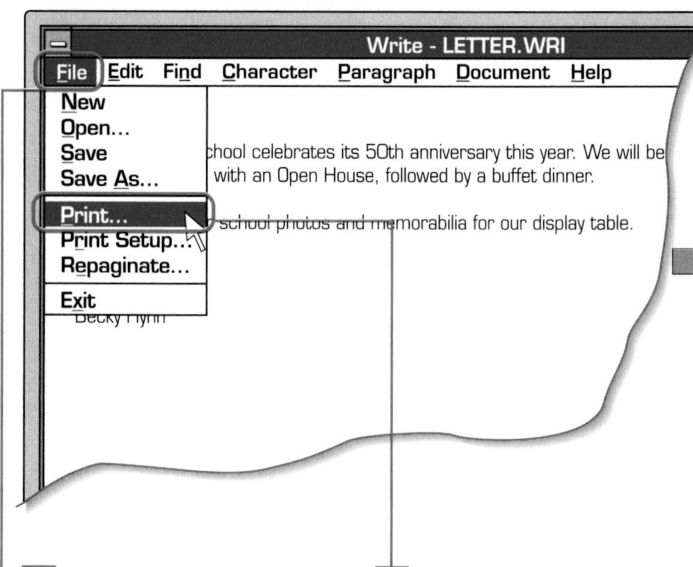

4 Move the mouse over **File** and then press the left button.

5 Move the mouse over **Print** and then press the left button.

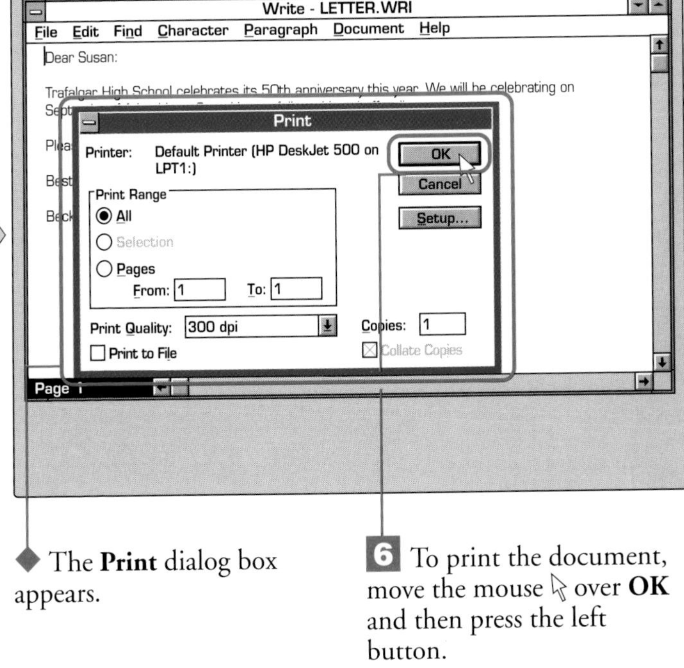

◆ The **Print** dialog box appears.

6 To print the document, move the mouse ↖ over **OK** and then press the left button.

START THE PRINT MANAGER

Start the Print Manager

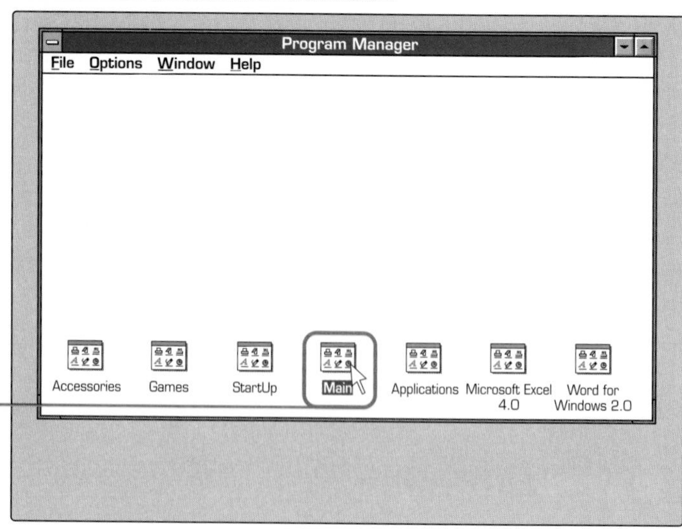

1 To open the **Main** group window, move the mouse over its icon and then quickly press the left button twice.

The Print Manager controls the printing of your documents. It enables you to cancel or pause printing.

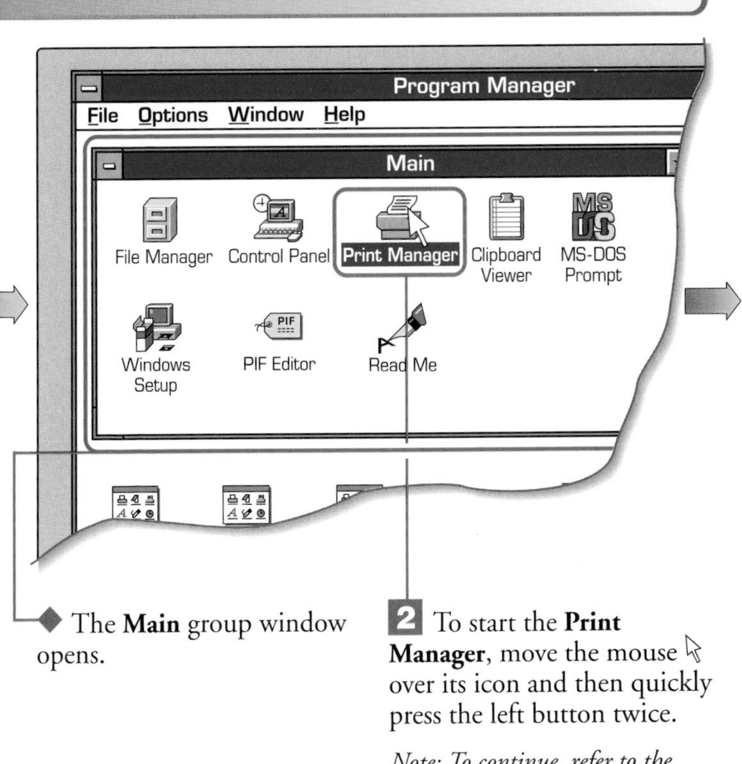

◆ The **Main** group window opens.

2 To start the **Print Manager**, move the mouse over its icon and then quickly press the left button twice.

Note: To continue, refer to the next page.

START THE PRINT MANAGER

Start the Print Manager (Continued)

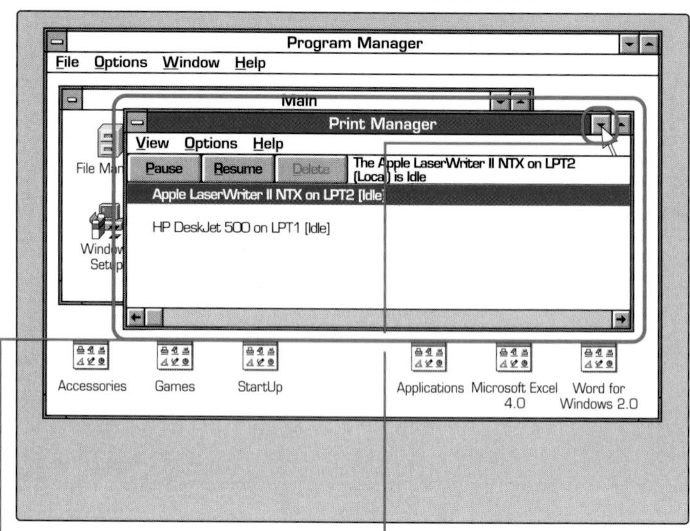

◆ The **Print Manager** window opens.

3 To reduce the **Print Manager** window to an icon, move the mouse over its **Minimize** button and then press the left button.

You can display the Print Manager as an icon on your screen. This lets you use the Print Manager at any time.

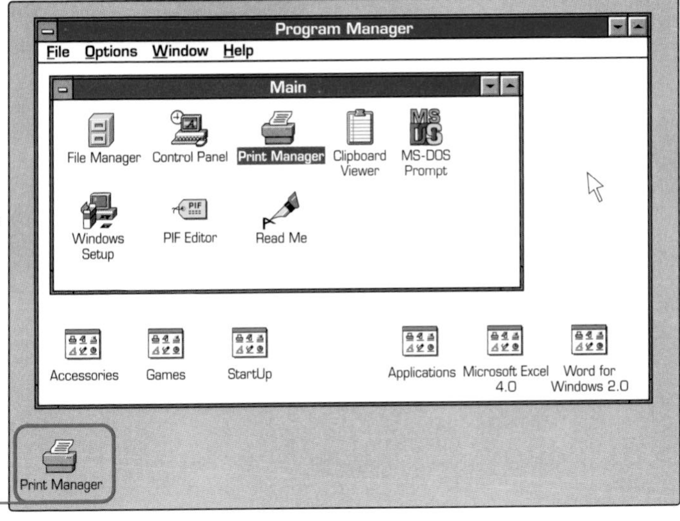

◆ The **Print Manager** window is reduced to an icon.

CANCEL A PRINT JOB

Cancel a Print Job

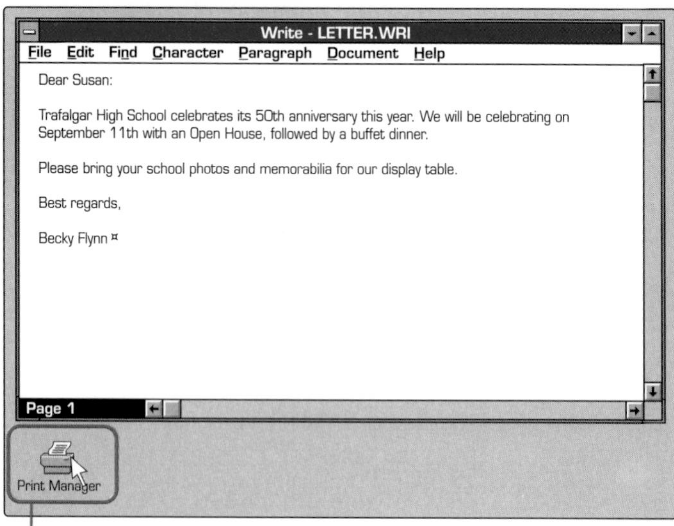

1 To open the **Print Manager** window, move the mouse over its icon and then quickly press the left button twice.

Note: To start the Print Manager, refer to page 210.

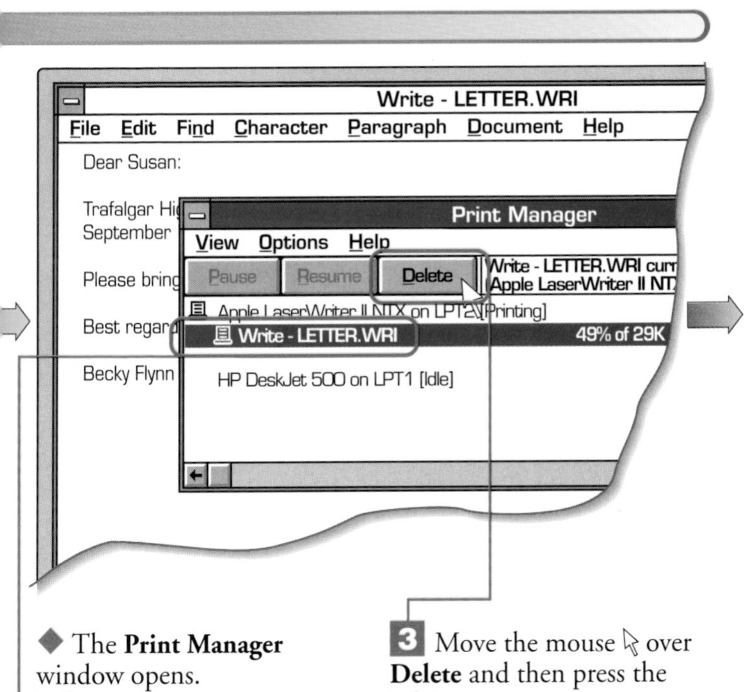

◆ The **Print Manager** window opens.

2 Move the mouse over the document you do not want to print and then press the left button.

3 Move the mouse over **Delete** and then press the left button.

Note: To continue, refer to the next page.

Cancel a Print Job (Continued)

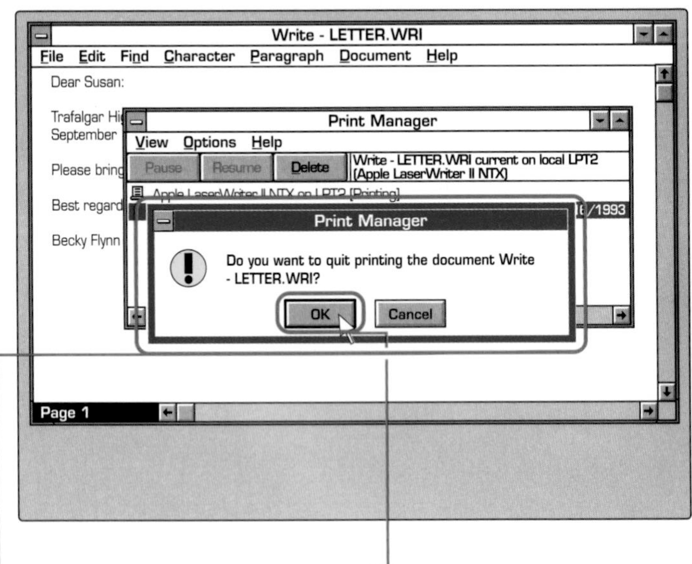

◆ This dialog box appears.

4 To quit printing the document, move the mouse over **OK** and then press the left button.

Note: To continue printing the document, move the mouse over ***Cancel*** *and then press the left button.*

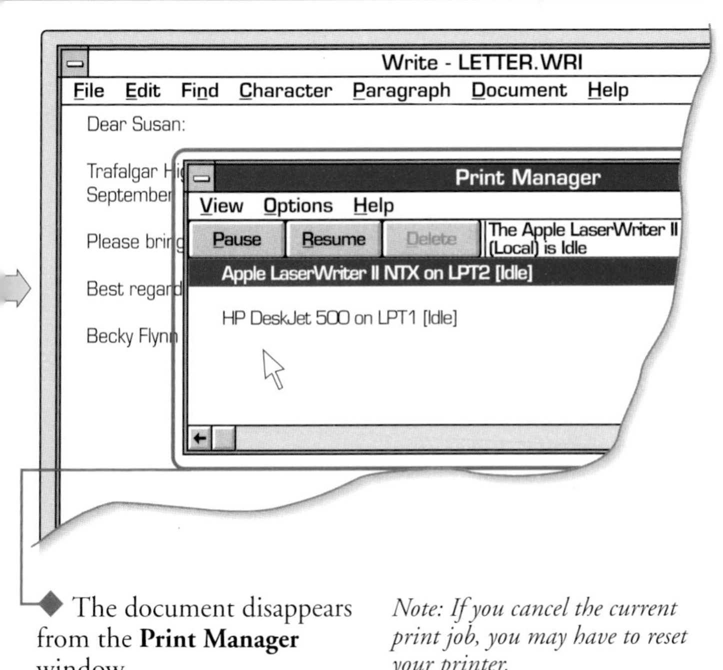

◆ The document disappears from the **Print Manager** window.

Note: If you cancel the current print job, you may have to reset your printer.

PAUSE A PRINT JOB

Pause a Print Job

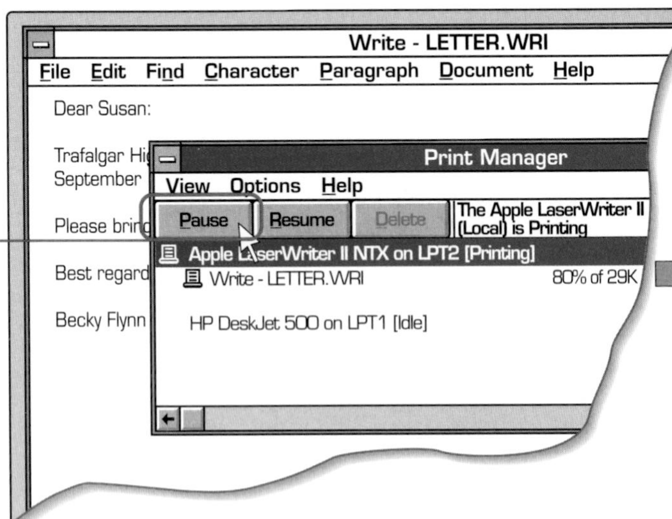

1 To pause the printing of a document, move the mouse over **Pause** and then press the left button.

Note: To start the Print Manager, refer to page 210.

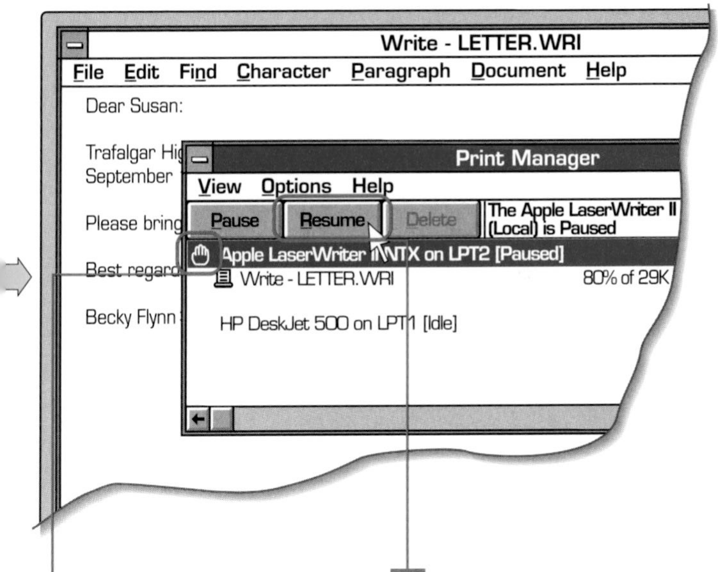

◆ The printer stops printing and a pause icon ( ) appears.

2 To start printing again, move the mouse over **Resume** and then press the left button.

OPEN THE CONTROL PANEL

You can use the Control Panel to change the Windows environment. The Control Panel lets you:

Open the Control Panel

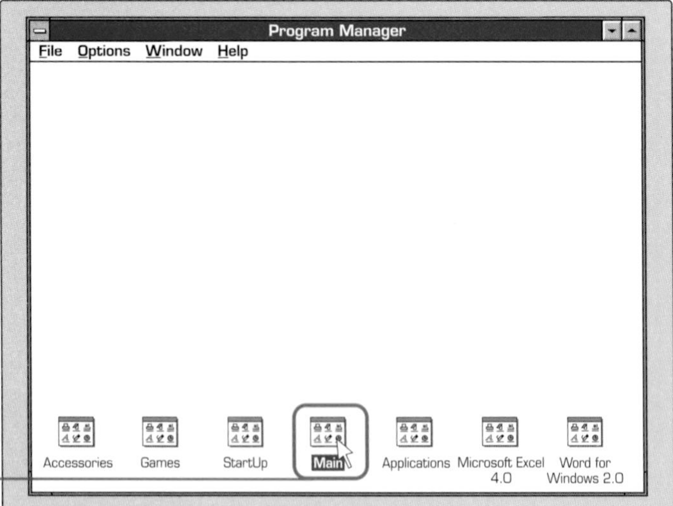

1 To open the **Main** group window, move the mouse over its icon and then quickly press the left button twice.

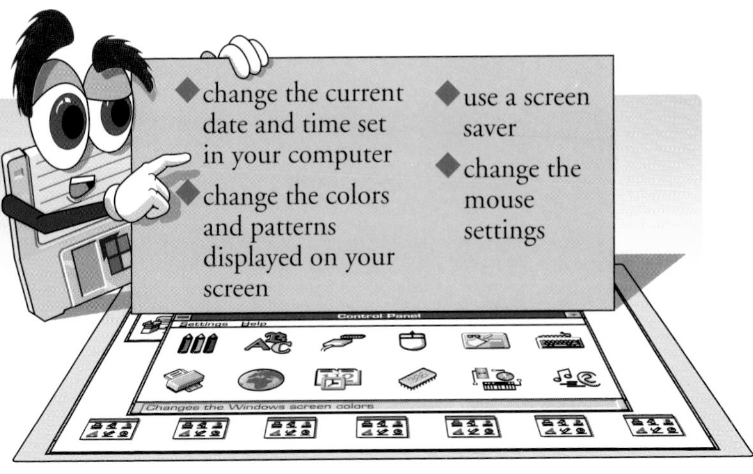

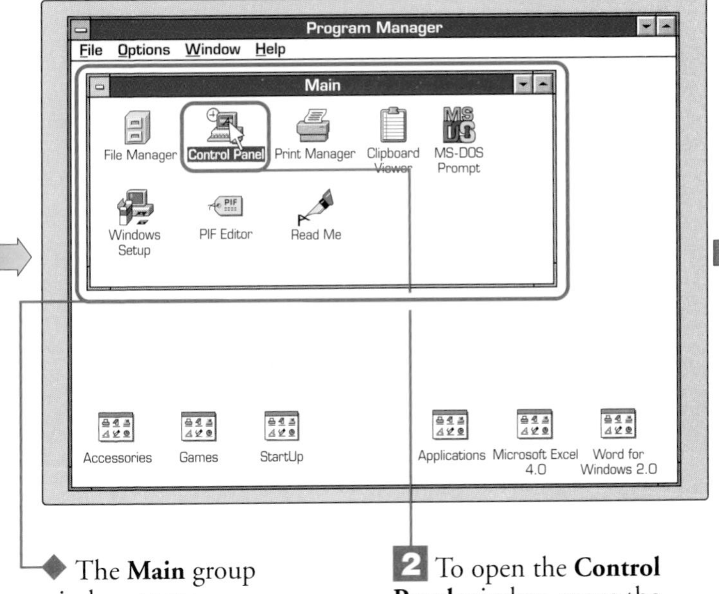

◆ The **Main** group window opens.

2 To open the **Control Panel** window, move the mouse over its icon and then quickly press the left button twice.

Note: To continue, refer to the next page.

OPEN THE CONTROL PANEL

Open the Control Panel (Continued)

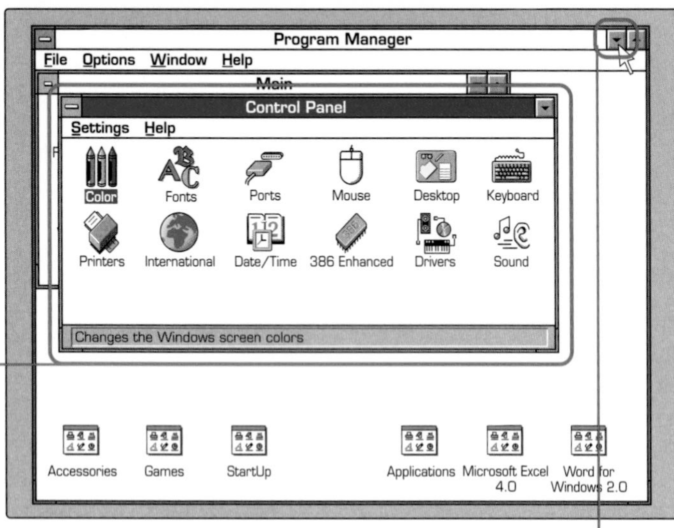

◆ The **Control Panel** window opens.

3 To reduce the **Program Manager** window to an icon, move the mouse over its **Minimize** button and then press the left button.

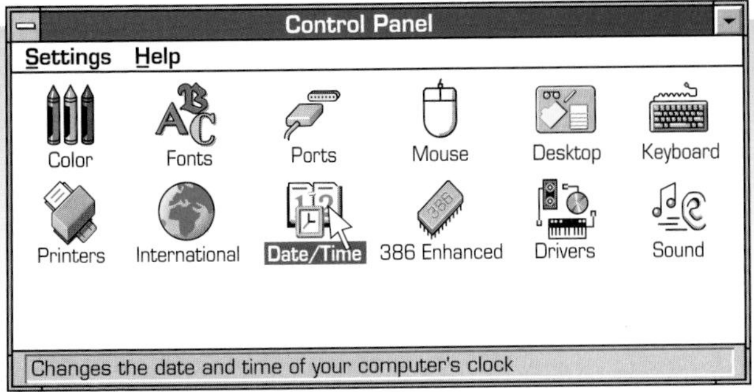

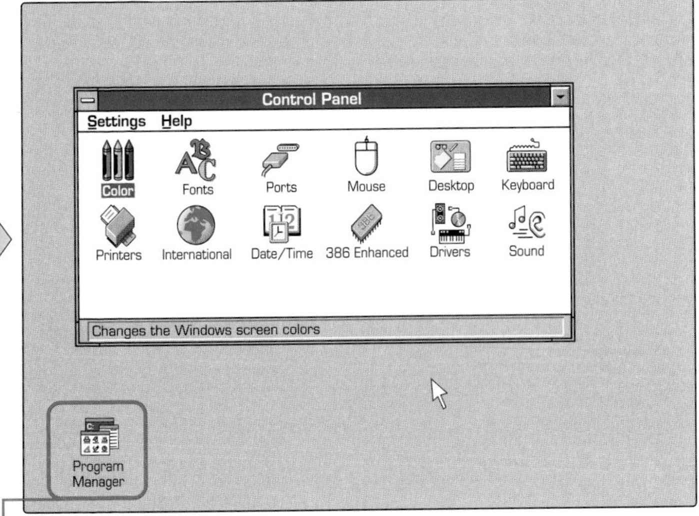

◆ The **Program Manager** window is reduced to an icon.

*Note: You can restore the **Program Manager** icon to a window at any time. To do so, move the mouse over the icon and then quickly press the left button twice.*

CHANGE DATE AND TIME

Change Date and Time

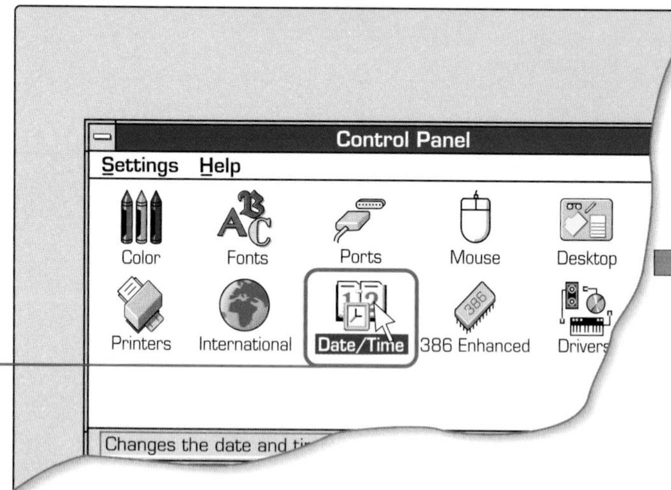

1 To start the **Date/Time** program, move the mouse over its icon and then quickly press the left button twice.

*Note: To open the **Control Panel**, refer to page 220.*

You can change the date and time set in your computer. This is important if you want to save files using the correct date and time or if you are using time sensitive programs like Calendar.

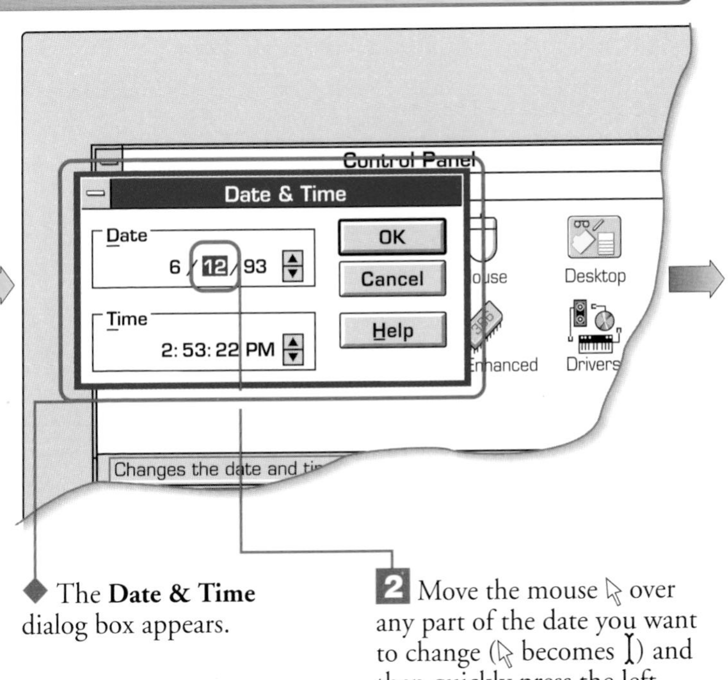

◆ The **Date & Time** dialog box appears.

2 Move the mouse over any part of the date you want to change (becomes I) and then quickly press the left button twice. The item becomes highlighted.

Note: To continue, refer to the next page.

CHANGE DATE AND TIME

Change Date and Time (Continued)

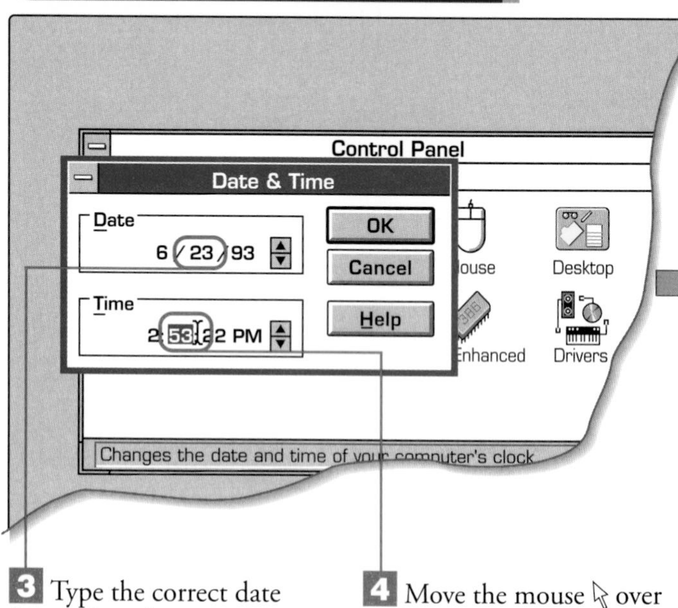

3 Type the correct date (example: **23**).

4 Move the mouse ⇖ over any part of the time you want to change (⇖ becomes I) and then quickly press the left button twice. The item becomes highlighted.

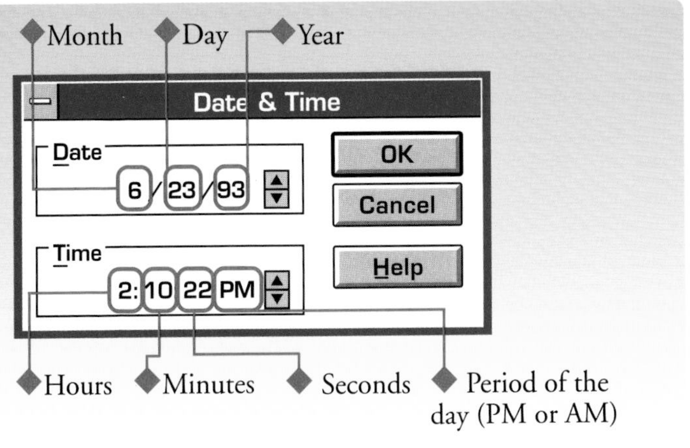

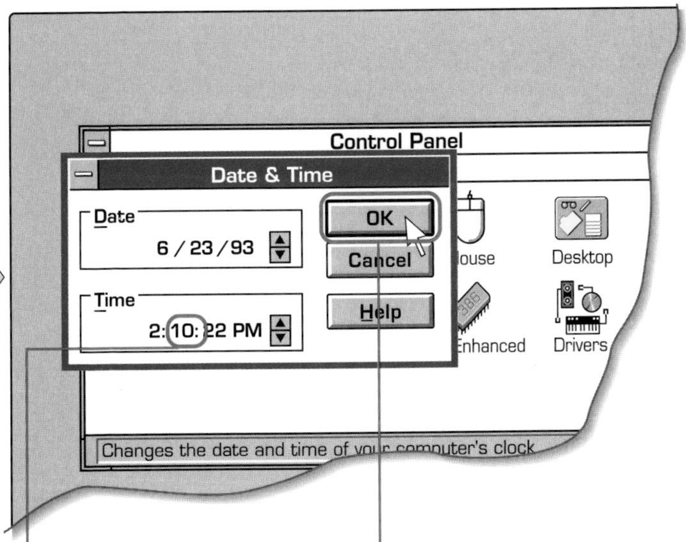

5 Type the correct time (example: **10**).

6 To confirm the date and time changes, move the mouse over **OK** and then press the left button.

CHANGE SCREEN COLORS

Change Screen Colors

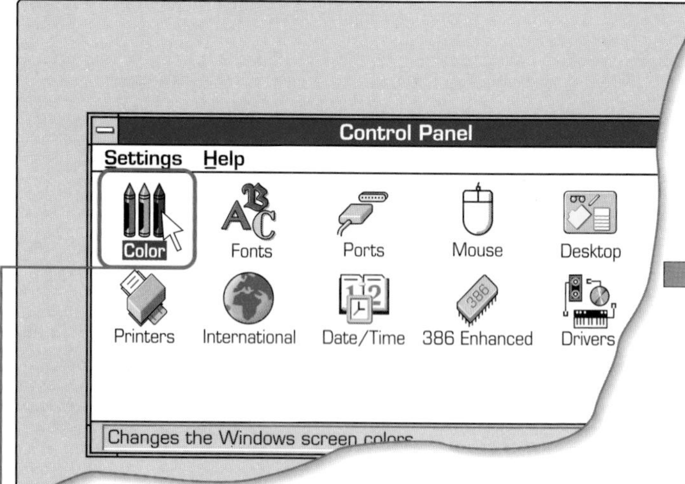

1 To start the **Color** program, move the mouse over its icon and then quickly press the left button twice.

*Note: To open the **Control Panel**, refer to page 220.*

You can change the colors that Windows displays on your screen.

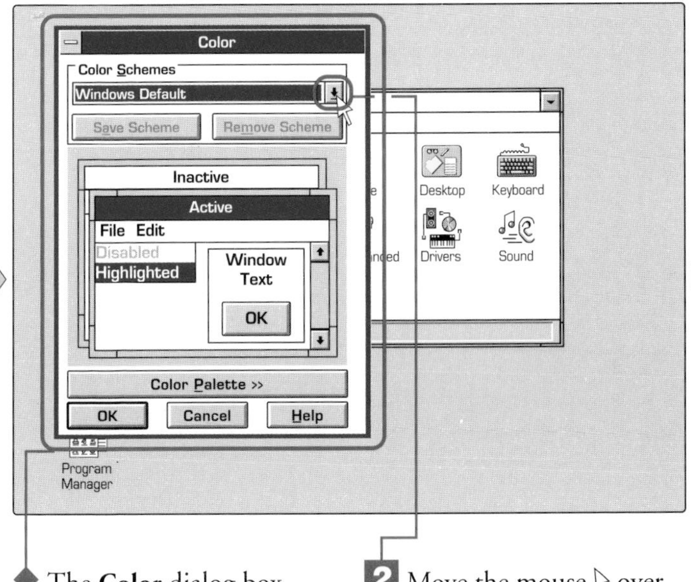

◆ The **Color** dialog box appears.

2 Move the mouse over the arrow under **Color Schemes** and then press the left button.

Note: To continue, refer to the next page.

CHANGE SCREEN COLORS

Change Screen Colors (Continued)

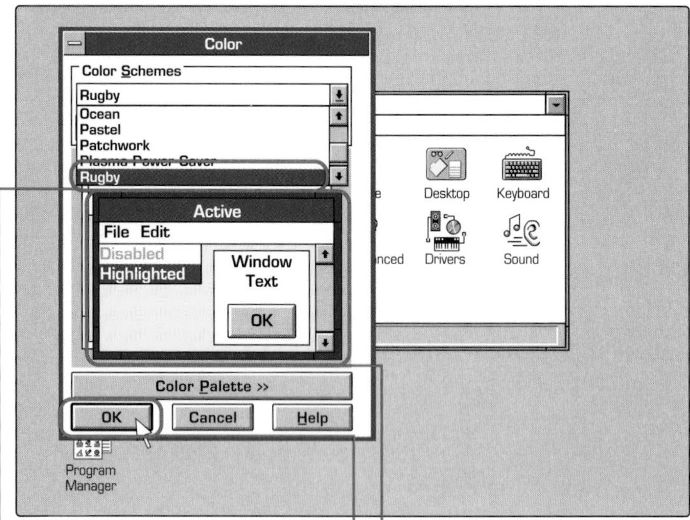

◆ A list of the available color schemes appears.

3 Press ↓ or ↑ on your keyboard until you highlight the color scheme you want to use (example: **Rugby**).

◆ Windows displays a sample of the highlighted color scheme.

4 To select the highlighted color scheme, move the mouse over **OK** and then press the left button.

Tip:

If you have a portable computer with a monochrome screen, use one of the following color schemes:

LCD Default Screen Settings

LCD Reversed - Dark

LCD Reversed - Light

These color schemes provide maximum visibility.

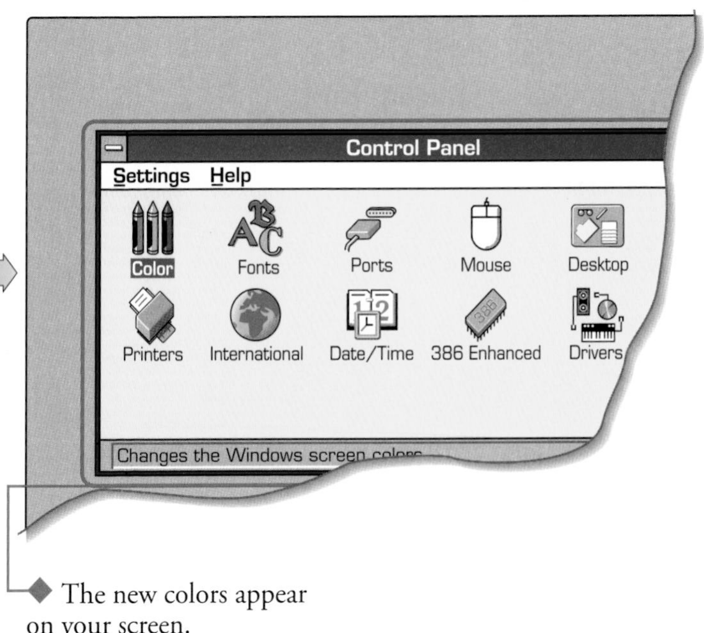

◆ The new colors appear on your screen.

ADD WALLPAPER

You can decorate your screen and impress your friends by adding wallpaper.

Add Wallpaper

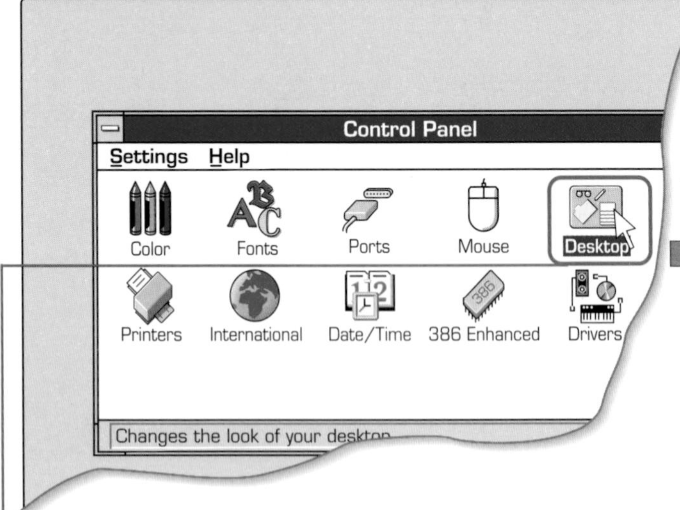

1 To start the **Desktop** program, move the mouse over its icon and then quickly press the left button twice.

*Note: To open the **Control Panel**, refer to page 220.*

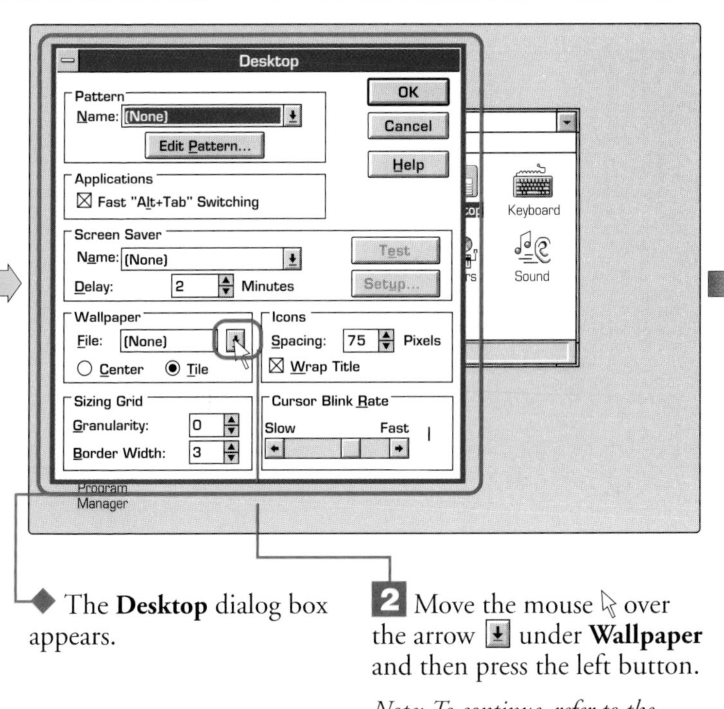

◆ The **Desktop** dialog box appears.

2 Move the mouse over the arrow under **Wallpaper** and then press the left button.

Note: To continue, refer to the next page.

ADD WALLPAPER

Add Wallpaper (Continued)

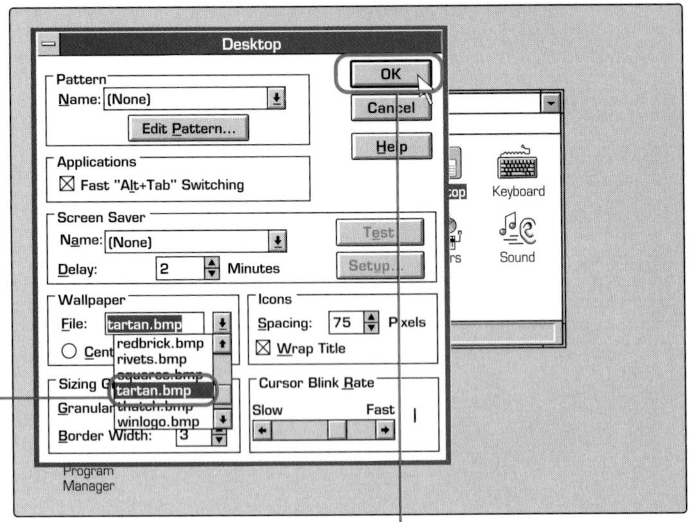

◆ A list of the available wallpaper patterns appears.

3 Press ↓ or ↑ on your keyboard until you highlight the wallpaper you want to use (example: **tartan.bmp**).

4 To select the highlighted wallpaper, move the mouse ↖ over **OK** and then press the left button.

Tip:

Displaying wallpaper on your screen reduces the memory available to run other applications. It may also slow down your computer.

If you start to run out of memory or your computer slows down, return to the **(None)** wallpaper option.

◆ The new wallpaper appears on your screen.

USE A SCREEN SAVER

If you do not use your computer for a certain period of time, you can have a screen saver automatically appear. A screen saver is a picture that constantly moves on your screen.

Use a Screen Saver

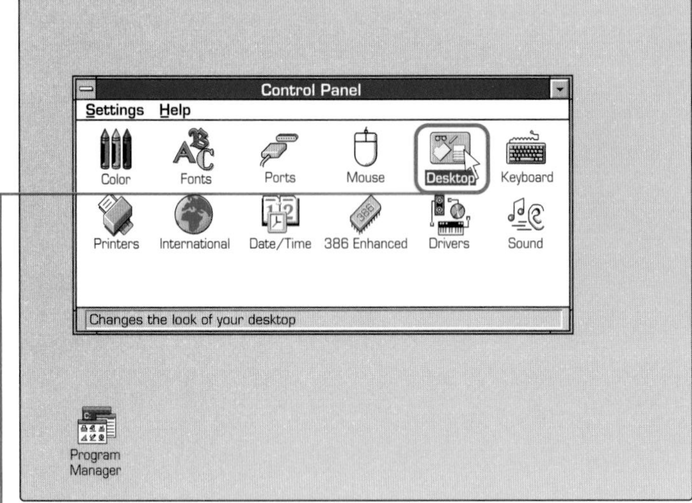

1 To start the **Desktop** program, move the mouse over its icon and then quickly press the left button twice.

*Note: To open the **Control Panel**, refer to page 220.*

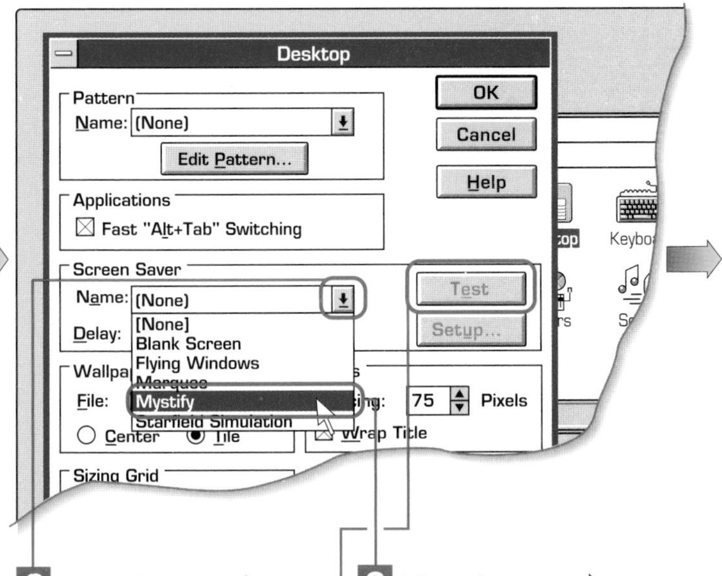

2 Move the mouse over the arrow under **Screen Saver** and then press the left button.

◆ A list of the available screen savers appears.

3 Move the mouse over the screen saver you want to use (example: **Mystify**) and then press the left button.

4 To see a demonstration of the screen saver you selected, move the mouse over **Test** and then press the left button.

Note: To continue, refer to the next page.

USE A SCREEN SAVER

Screen savers eliminate "screen burn" which occurs when an image appears in a fixed position for a long period of time.

Use a Screen Saver (Continued)

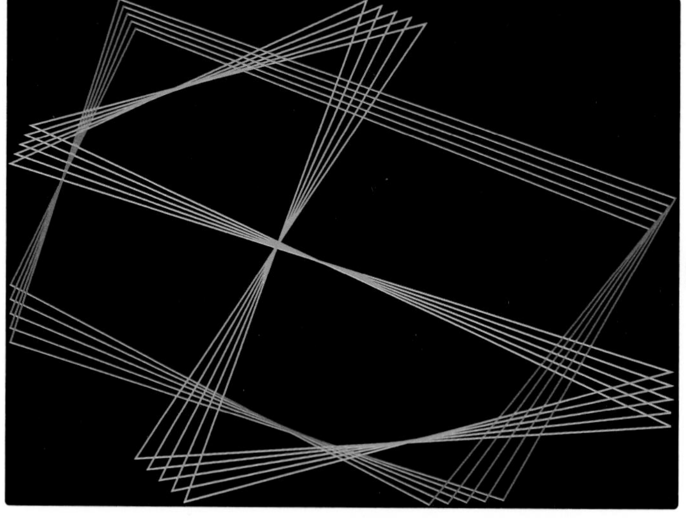

◆ A demonstration of the screen saver appears.

5 Move the mouse on your desk to stop the demonstration.

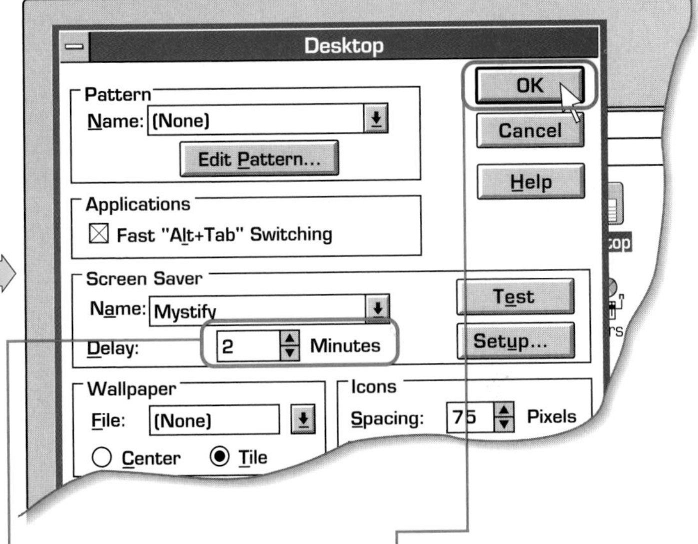

◆ This box displays the number of minutes of inactivity before the screen saver appears.

6 To change the delay time, move the mouse over the box beside **Delay:** and then quickly press the left button twice. Then type a new delay time.

7 To select the screen saver, move the mouse over **OK** and then press the left button.

CHANGE MOUSE SETTINGS

You can change the way your mouse works by customizing its speed, appearance and function.

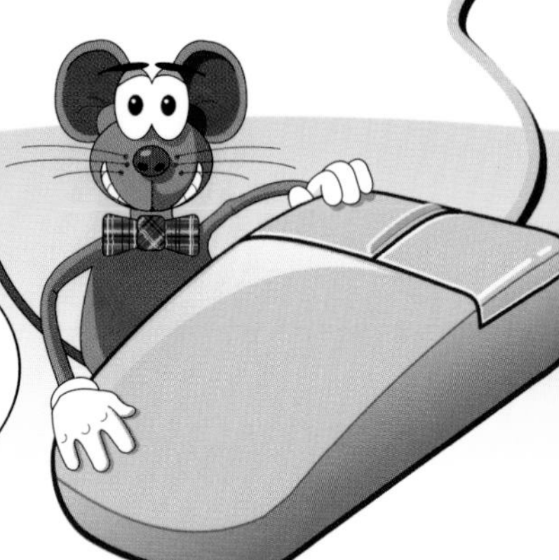

Change Mouse Settings

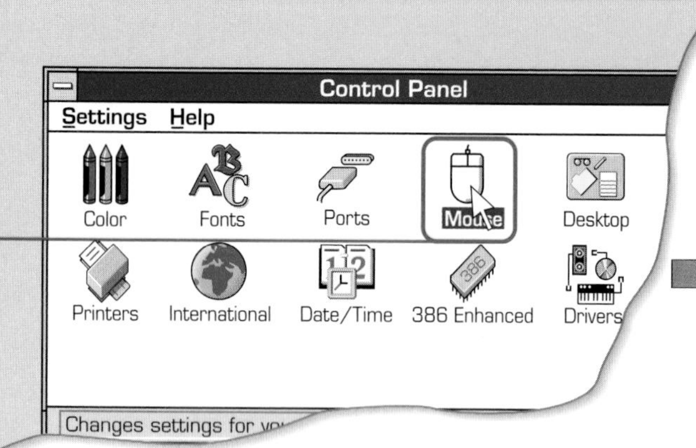

1 To start the **Mouse** program, move the mouse ↖ over its icon and then quickly press the left button twice.

*Note: To open the **Control Panel**, refer to page 220.*

Tip:

To test a new double-click speed, move the mouse over **TEST** in the **Mouse** dialog box and then quickly press the left button twice. **TEST** becomes **TEST** if you clicked at the correct speed.

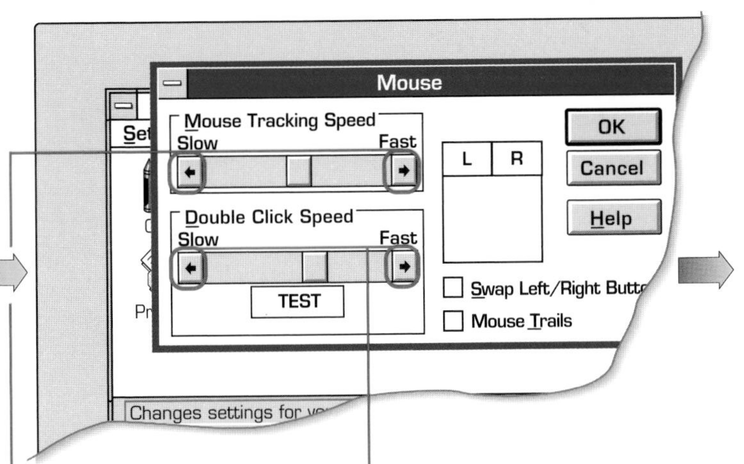

Change mouse speed

2 To change the speed of the mouse on your screen, move the mouse over the left or right arrow and then press the left button.

*Note: The changes you make in the **Mouse** dialog box take effect immediately.*

Change double click speed

3 To change the speed that Windows registers a double-click, move the mouse over the left or right arrow and then press the left button.

Note: To continue, refer to the next page.

CHANGE MOUSE SETTINGS

If you have a portable computer, the Mouse Trails option can improve the visibility of the mouse on your screen.

Change Mouse Settings (Continued)

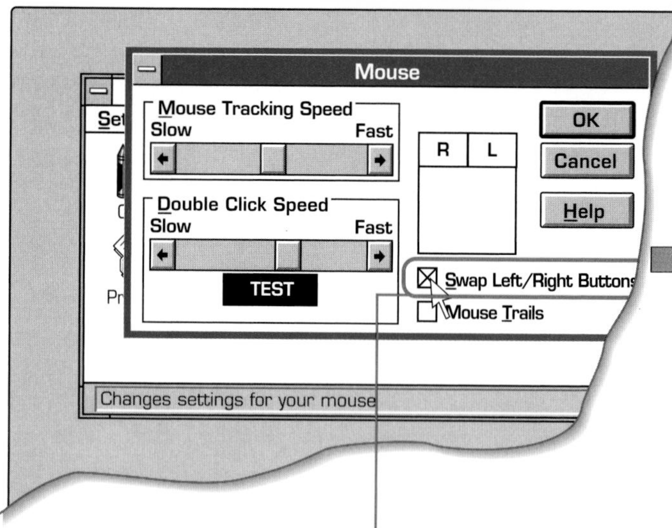

Swap left/right buttons

◆ If you are left-handed, you may find the mouse easier to use if you switch the functions of the left and right mouse buttons.

4 Move the mouse ⇖ over this box and then press the left button (☐ becomes ☒).

◆ You must now use the right mouse button to select commands.

Tip:

◆ The **Mouse** dialog box displayed on your screen may be different than shown below. There are many versions of mouse software available and each one displays a different **Mouse** dialog box.

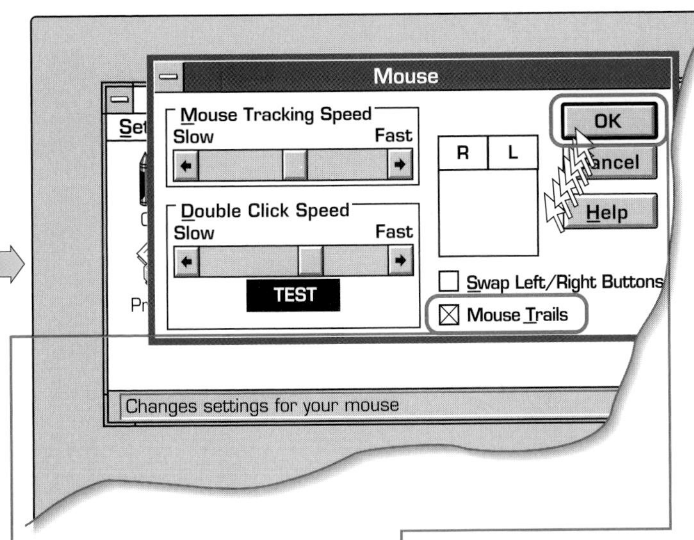

Mouse trails

5 To leave a trail of mouse pointers as you move around your screen, move the mouse ⇖ over this box and then press the left button (☐ becomes ☒).

6 To confirm the changes you made, move the mouse ⇖ over **OK** and then press the left button.

*Note: To cancel the changes, move the mouse ⇖ over **Cancel** and then press the left button.*

IDG BOOKS' ... FOR DUMMIES™ SERIES

Find out why over 11 million computer users love IDG'S ...FOR DUMMIES BOOKS!

"I laughed and learned..."
Arlene J. Peterson, Rapid City, South Dakota

DOS FOR DUMMIES™, 2nd EDITION

by Dan Gookin
This fun and easy DOS primer has taught millions of readers how to learn DOS! A #1 bestseller for over 56 weeks!

ISBN: 1-878058-75-4
$16.95 USA
$21.95 Canada
£15.99 UK

PCs FOR DUMMIES™, 2nd EDITION

by Dan Gookin & Andy Rathbone
This #1 bestselling reference is the perfect companion for the computer phobic.

ISBN: 1-56884-078-0
$16.95 USA
$21.95 Canada
£15.99 UK

WINDOWS 3.1 FOR DUMMIES™, 2nd EDITION

by Andy Rathbone
Learn the Windows interface with this bestselling reference.

ISBN: 1-56884-182-5
$16.95 USA
$21.95 Canada
£15.99 UK

EXCEL FOR DUMMIES™, 2nd EDITION

by Greg Harvey
Updated, expanded—The easy-to-use reference to Excel 5 features and commands.

ISBN: 1-56884-050-0
$16.95 USA
$21.95 Canada
£15.99 UK

THE INTERNET FOR DUMMIES™
ISBN: 1-56884-024-1
$19.95 USA/$26.95 Canada
£18.99 UK

MACs FOR DUMMIES™, 2nd EDITION
ISBN: 1-56884-051-9
$19.95 USA/$26.95 Canada
£18.99 UK

WORDPERFECT FOR DUMMIES™
ISBN: 1-878058-52-5
$16.95 USA/$21.95 Canada
£15.99 UK

UPGRADING AND FIXING PCs FOR DUMMIES™
ISBN: 1-56884-002-0
$19.95 USA/$26.95 Canada
£18.99 UK

WORD FOR WINDOWS FOR DUMMIES™
ISBN: 1-878058-86-X
$16.95 USA/$21.95 Canada
£15.99 UK

WORDPERFECT 6 FOR DUMMIES™
ISBN: 1-878058-77-0
$16.95 USA/$21.95 Canada
£15.99 UK

1-2-3 FOR DUMMIES™
ISBN: 1-878058-60-6
$16.95 USA/$21.95 Canada
£15.99 UK

UNIX FOR DUMMIES™
ISBN: 1-878058-58-4
$19.95 USA/$26.95 Canada
£18.99 UK

For more information or to order by mail, call 1-800-762-2974. Call for a free catalog! For volume discounts and special orders, please call Tony Real, Special Sales, at 415-312-0644. For International sales and distribution information, please call our authorized distributors:

UNITED KINGDOM Transworld
44-81-231-6661

AUSTRALIA Woodslane Pty Ltd.
61-2-979-5944

SIMPLIFIED

WINDOWS 3.1 SIMPLIFIED

By: maranGraphics
ISBN: 1-56884-652-5
$14.99 USA
£13.99 UK

COMPUTERS SIMPLIFIED

By: maranGraphics
ISBN: 1-56884-651-7
$14.99 USA
£13.99 UK

WORD 6 FOR WINDOWS SIMPLIFIED

By: maranGraphics
ISBN: 1-56884-659-2
$14.99 USA
£13.99 UK

MS-DOS 6.2 SIMPLIFIED

By: maranGraphics
ISBN: 1-56884-653-3
$14.99 USA
£13.99 UK

SIMPLIFIED EXPANDED

WINDOWS 3.1 SIMPLIFIED EXPANDED

By: maranGraphics
ISBN: 1-56884-654-1
$19.99 USA
£18.99 UK

EXCEL 5 SIMPLIFIED EXPANDED

By: maranGraphics
ISBN: 1-56884-664-9
$19.99 USA
£18.99 UK

WORD 6 FOR WINDOWS SIMPLIFIED EXPANDED

By: maranGraphics
ISBN: 1-56884-660-6
$19.99 USA
£18.99 UK

VISUAL POCKETGUIDE

WINDOWS 3.1 VISUAL POCKETGUIDE

By: maranGraphics
ISBN: 1-56884-650-9
$14.99 USA
£13.99 UK

EXCEL 5 VISUAL POCKETGUIDE

By: maranGraphics
ISBN: 1-56884-667-3
$14.99 USA
£13.99 UK

WORD 6 FOR WINDOWS VISUAL POCKETGUIDE

By: maranGraphics
ISBN: 1-56884-666-5
$14.99 USA
£13.99 UK

"If you're someone new to computers and 'all thumbs' or just scared of the machines, this series of books will gently guide you through. Nothing could be clearer. They are made for novices."
Peter McWilliams, Nationally Syndicated Columnist

"This full-color illustrated guide to Windows is a must-have, whether you're a new Windows user or just one looking for easy-to-learn Windows shortcuts."
Inside Microsoft Windows, The Cobb Group

"...maranGraphics is the greatest thing that has happened to computers since the invention of the PC."
Jim Van Speybroeck, Data Processing Digest

Order Form

Order Center: (800) 762-2974
(8 a.m.-5 p.m., EST, weekdays) or (317) 895-5260

For Fastest Service: Photocopy This Order Form and FAX it to: (317) 895-5299

Qty.	ISBN	Title	Price	Total

Shipping & Handling Charges

Subtotal	U.S.	International	International Air Mail
Up to $20.00	Add $3.00	Add $4.00	Add $10.00
$20.01-40.00	$4.00	$5.00	$20.00
$40.01-60.00	$5.00	$6.00	$25.00
$60.01-80.00	$6.00	$8.00	$35.00
Over $80.00	$7.00	$10.00	$50.00

In U.S., shipping is UPS ground or equivalent.
For Rush shipping call (800) 762-2974.

Subtotal ________

CA residents add applicable sales tax ________

IN and MA residents add 5% sales tax ________

IL residents add 6.25% sales tax ________

RI residents add 7% sales tax ________

Shipping ________

Total ________

Ship to:

Name ______________________ Daytime Phone ______________________

Address ____

City/State/Zip ____

Payment: ❑ Check to IDG Books (US Funds Only) ❑ Visa ❑ Mastercard ❑ American Express

Card# ______________________ Exp.__________ Signature______________

Please send this order form to: IDG Books, 3250 North Post Road, Suite 140, Indianapolis, IN 46226. Allow up to 3 weeks for delivery. Thank you!

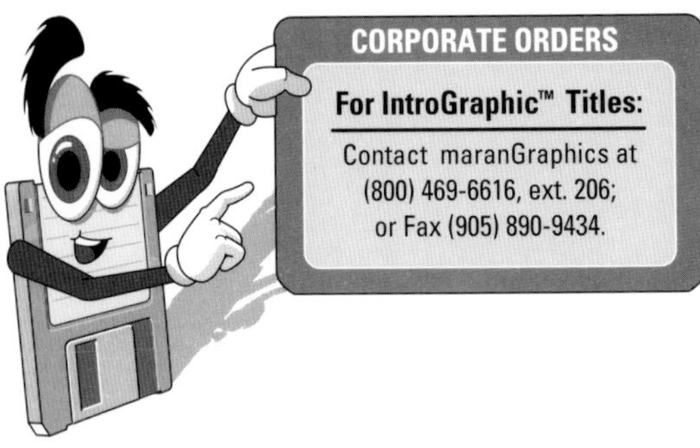

IDG BOOKS WORLDWIDE REGISTRATION CARD

Title of this book: **WINDOWS 3.1 VISUAL POCKET GUIDE**

IDG BOOKS
THE WORLD OF COMPUTER KNOWLEDGE

My overall rating of this book:
❑ Very good [1] ❑ Good [2] ❑ Satisfactory [3] ❑ Fair [4] ❑ Poor [5]

How I first heard about this book:
❑ Found in bookstore; name: [6] ______
❑ Book review: [7] ______
❑ Advertisement: [8] ______
❑ Catalog: [9] ______
❑ Word of mouth; heard about book from friend, co-worker, etc.: [10]
❑ Other: [11] ______

What I liked most about this book: ______

What I would change, add, delete, etc., in future editions of this book: ______

Other comments: ______

Number of computer books I purchase in a year: ❑ 1 [12] ❑ 2-5 [13] ❑ 6-10 [14] ❑ More than 10 [15]

I would characterize my computer skills as:
❑ Beginner [16] ❑ Intermediate [17] ❑ Advanced [18] ❑ Professional [19]

I use ❑ DOS [20] ❑ Windows [21] ❑ OS/2 [22] ❑ Unix [23] ❑ Macintosh [24] ❑ Other: [25] ______ (please specify)

I would be interested in new books on the following subjects:
(please check all that apply, and use the spaces provided to identify specific software)

❑ Word processing: [26] ______ ❑ Spreadsheets: [27] ______
❑ Data bases: [28] ______ ❑ Desktop publishing: [29] ______
❑ File Utilities: [30] ______ ❑ Money management: [31] ______
❑ Networking: [32] ______ ❑ Programming languages: [33] ______
❑ Other: [34] ______

I use a PC at (please check all that apply): ❑ home [35] ❑ work [36] ❑ school [37] ❑ other: [38] ______
The disks I prefer to use are ❑ 5.25 [39] ❑ 3.5 [40] ❑ other: [41] ______

I have a CD ROM: ❑ yes [42] ❑ no [43]

I plan to buy or upgrade computer hardware this year: ❑ yes [44] ❑ no [45]

I plan to buy or upgrade computer software this year: ❑ yes [46] ❑ no [47]

Name: ______ Business title: [48] ______
Type of Business: [49] ______
Address (❑ home [50] ❑ work [51]/Company name: ______)
Street/Suite# ______
City [52]/State [53]/Zipcode [54]: ______ Country [55] ______

❑ **I liked this book!**
You may quote me by name in future IDG Books Worldwide promotional materials.

My daytime phone number is ______

YES!

Please keep me informed about IDG's World of Computer Knowledge. Send me the latest IDG Books catalog.